BEYOND MODERNISM
AND POSTMODERNISM

BEYOND MODERNISM AND POSTMODERNISM

Essays on the Politics of Culture

Maurice R. Berube

BERGIN & GARVEY
Westport, Connecticut • London

Library of Congress Cataloging-in-Publication Data

Berube, Maurice R.
    Beyond modernism and postmodernism : essays on the politics of culture / Maurice
R. Berube.
        p.   cm.
    Includes bibliographical references and index.
    ISBN 0–89789–805–2 (alk. paper)
        1. Culture—Study and teaching.   2. Culture—Political aspects.   3.
    Postmodernism—United States.   4. Educational change—United States.   5.
    Intellectuals—United States—Political activity.   6. United States—Intellectual life.
    7. United States—Politics and government.   I. Title.
    HM623 .B47   2002
    306—dc21   2001037666

British Library Cataloguing in Publication Data is available.

Library of Congress Catalog Card Number: 2001037666
ISBN: 0–89789–805–2

First published in 2002

Bergin & Garvey, 88 Post Road West, Westport, CT 06881
An imprint of Greenwood Publishing Group, Inc.
www.greenwood.com

Printed in the United States of America

The paper used in this book complies with the
Permanent Paper Standard issued by the National
Information Standards Organization (Z39.48–1984).

10 9 8 7 6 5 4 3 2 1

COPYRIGHT ACKNOWLEDGMENTS

The author and publisher gratefully acknowledge permission for use of the following material:

Maurice R. Berube, "Arts and Education." *The Clearing House*, January/February 1999. Used by permission of *The Clearing House* and Heldref Publications.

Maurice R. Berube, "His Greatest Paintings Produced a Spiritual Calm—One That Jackson Pollack Was Never Able to Share." *The Chronicle of Higher Education*, January 15, 1999. Used by permission of *The Chronicle of Higher Education*.

Maurice R. Berube, "The Politics of National Standards." *The Clearing House*, January/February 1996. Used by permission of *The Clearing House* and Heldref Publications.

Maurice R. Berube, "Pollock: The Artist and the Film." *Port Folio Weekly*, March 20, 2000. This review was originally published in *Port Folio Weekly*, an alternative newspaper serving Southeastern Virginia.

Maurice R. Berube, "The Post-Millennium Blues: Is It the End of Education Also?" *Education Week* 19, no. 31 (April 12, 2000). Reprinted with permission from *Education Week*.

Maurice R. Berube, "A Teacher's Legacy." *Education Week* 16, no. 20 (February 12, 1997). Reprinted with permission from *Education Week*.

Diane Ravitch, *The Trouble Crusade: American Education 1945–1980*. New York: Basic Books, 1983. Used by permission of Perseus Books Group.

Interview by author with Janet Lyon.

For my wife, Clair T. Berube, for her love

And for my granddaughter, Marie Lucienne Boyer

Contents

Preface: Connections

This collection of essays, some new, others published in the last few years, has as its theme the relationship of intellect to schooling to culture. The essays were written independently of one another; yet like a series of Mark Rothko paintings, they establish a common theme that can be read as variations on that theme.

As one born during the Great Depression in the United States, I am more comfortable with the modernist expression of a high art, at times a spiritual art. My son Michael Bérubé, a professor of English, (as you will see in some of these essays) is immersed in a postmodern sensibility of popular culture. Besides this major difference between *père et fils*, there is the minor one of acute accents. I dispensed with the family use of the accents as a young Catholic radical fighting corruption in trade unions during the 1950s. I did not feel that Maurice R. Bérubé would exactly inspire confidence in a caucus of Teamster members. My children kept the accents.

The last hall of the twentieth century belongs to postmodernism, the first half to modernism. These essays probe the political connection of modernism and postmodernism. I arrived at the conclusion that every aspect of life has a politics. There is a politics of art, of literature, of religion, of schooling, of the intellect; in short, of culture. In the United States that politics is often a protest politics. In 1950, the "irascible eighteen," a group of abstract expressionists, protested the exclusion of their

art in the Metropolitan Museum of Art in New York with a letter to the
New York Times. In the 1980s, similarly, a group of writers protested the
denial of the Pulitzer Prize to the African American novelist Toni Morrison. The Beat poet Allen Ginsberg remarked famously that his friend
and colleague Jack Kerouac "never understood the politics of literature."
These examples are of a modernist politics of protest; postmodern politics is aimed at changing the hearts and minds of people. A line in a Bob
Dylan song states that "I gave her my heart, but she wanted my soul."

   Following the postmodern example of narrative, I have inserted my
own experience (sparingly I hope) where it has bearing on the topic at
hand. I was a public intellectual publishing in intellectual journals of
opinion long before that term was applied to my son as well as to others.
I was acquainted with some of the figures who are named in these essays. Juxtaposing my thinking with theirs, I feel, clarifies the debate
somewhat. And that debate is over cultural politics. I hope the reader
will find as much satisfaction in reading these essays as I have had in
writing them.

   Special thanks to my editors at Greenwood Publishing: Dr. James T.
Sabin, Vice-President and Director of Academic Publishing; Frank Saun-
ders, production editor, and Marilyn A. Perlberg, copy editor.

PART I

INTELLECT

1

The Rise of the Postmodern Intellectual

Intellectuals in America have historically been embattled in their attempts to "speak truth to power." Intellectuals originated outside the academy, and they constantly battled a pervasive strain of anti-intellectualism in the United States. Their ranks were few, their publishing outlets consigned to a small readership. They functioned not as a group, or a class, but as individuals. Their goal was clearly to speak truth to power, to influence public policy. That was the modernist canon.

By the close of the twentieth century, intellectuals changed focus and location. Instead of practical politics, they preached a gospel of cultural politics. Instead of influencing legislation or public policy, they sought to change the hearts and minds of a larger public—to convert the masses rather than political elites. They no longer functioned in small intellectual magazines or as bohemian freelancers; they became university academics with expertise in narrow disciplines. They introduced the academic discipline of "cultural studies."

In this chapter I will describe the rise of the American intellectual in his/her various permutations and compare the policy-oriented modernist intellectual to the cultural-politics postmodern intellectual.

ANTI-INTELLECTUALISM IN AMERICA

The sad fact is that there is a powerful strain of anti-intellectualism in America. For example, in the 1992 election both George Bush and Bill

Clinton avoided presenting themselves to the American public as the smart products of Ivy League universities that they are. They purposely dumbed themselves down. Bush told a seasoned reporter, Gail Sheehy, that he could not recall any books that influenced him, prompting Sheehy to write that Bush "was not fired up by ideas."[1] On his part, Clinton at the nominating convention denigrated his schooling at Georgetown, Oxford, and Yale Law School as not commensurate with the wisdom of his grandfather, who barely graduated from elementary school.

Even Thomas Jefferson in his lifetime was accused by his political foes of being a "cultural elitist". In America today, the intellectual is too often portrayed as an object of ridicule in films and television; as an "egghead" at best, and a "nerd" at worst. This is not the case in Europe where political leaders such as François Mitterrand, former president of France, took pride in his many books, and Vaclav Havel, former president of Czechoslovakia, enjoyed his fame as an accomplished playwright.

In his classic 1963 study *Anti-Intellectualism in American Life*, historian Richard Hofstadter ably defined the problem. "The intellectual class," he wrote, "is of necessity an elite in manner of thinking and functioning."[2] Any form of elitism, Hofstadter argued, cuts against the grain of "democratic institutions and the egalitarian sentiments of this country."[3] In other words, Americans are more comfortable with ordinary Joes than brainiac Einsteins.

How smart do you have to be to be president of the United States? The question was raised once again in the 2000 presidential election. By all accounts, George W. Bush, the Republican candidate, appeared to be a dim bulb whose extemporaneous speeches resounded with malaprops and bad grammar. A George W. sampler included gems like these: On John McCain: "You can't take the high horse and then claim the low road." To working people: "I know how hard it is to be put food on your family." On the economy: "You want to make the pie higher."[4] Moreover, according to one of his aides, George W.'s favorite intellectual pastime is watching ESPN, the all-sports television channel.

By contrast, Al Gore, the Democratic candidate, had the appearance of an intellectual. A former reporter, he wrote a weighty tome on the environment generally regarded as substantive by scholars. He preferred the company of intellectuals and culture stars. In an admiring portrait in *The New Yorker* magazine, Gore was described as "never happier than with meeting the type of person he admires most—not a politician but an intellectual, cultural, or spiritual figure who has thought about the world in a new way, such as Carl Sagan, the astronomer, or Deborah Tannen, the linguist . . . or . . . The Dalai Lama or Stephen Hawking, the theoretical physicist."[5] Gore wrote his own acceptance speech for the

Democratic Convention, whereas George W. had his team of ghostwriters pen his.

Both are Ivy League graduates—George W. from his father's alma mater Yale, and Gore from Harvard. George W. slept through the turbulent sixties, never participating in any campus politics, whereas Gore was active in many campus groups. Legend has it that George W.'s father, disconcerted by his son's lack of seriousness, reprimanded him by saying, "Why can't you be like Al Gore?"

With George W. as elected president of the United States, do we have cause to be nervous about the state of the union? Perhaps. But a plethora of intellectual lightweights have been U.S. presidents. For starters, consider Ronald Reagan, Gerald Ford, Franklin Delano Roosevelt, and Lyndon Johnson. Yet some of these chief executives were extremely successful. In my book *American Presidents and Education,* I identified two presidents who were truly "education presidents": Lyndon Johnson and Ronald Reagan. Both led large-scale educational reform movements.

On the other hand, there have been truly brilliant men whose stewardship was questionable. Consider Thomas Jefferson, Woodrow Wilson, and Herbert Hoover, all published writers of significant books. Yet Jefferson's gravestone, for example, neglects to mention that he was president. Instead he is identified as author of the Declaration of Independence and founder of the University of Virginia. Evidently Jefferson did not regard his presidency as one of his best efforts.

One of the keys to a successful presidency is having a talented staff upon which to rely. After that, one has to be able to make the right decision from the information the staff provides. FDR, Johnson, and Reagan depended heavily on an extremely bright and competent entourage. By contrast, Jimmy Carter was an especially intelligent chief executive whose staff was suspect. Consequently, his was a dysfunctional presidency.

Of course, the heart of the matter is how to define intelligence. The Harvard cognitive psychologist Howard Gardner adopts the Deweyean definition of intelligence as the ability to solve real problems in life. Gardner then proceeds to identify approximately eight separate intelligences, one of which he calls interpersonal intelligence: the ability to lead and manage people. Robert Steinberg, Gardner's friend at Yale, has developed a practical intelligence test for executives in business, which has been validated concerning Gardner's theory of interpersonal intelligence. In other words, in Gardner's rubric there may be more smarts than book smarts.

Which begs the question: How smart does one have to be in order to be president of the United States? The historical record may give us an answer. According to a 1996 poll of major historians and presidential biographers, only *three* presidents met the standard for truly great presidents: Abraham Lincoln, George Washington, and Franklin Delano Roosevelt—none of whom could be classified as an intellectual.[6]

WHAT (AND WHO) IS AN INTELLECTUAL?

Since the introduction of the concept of intellectual, which dates back to Voltaire and the *philosophes engagés* of the Enlightenment, there have been a number of definitions of intellectual. Simply put, an intellectual is one who deals in ideas. Intellectuals, then, constitute a class that encompasses both scholars and those outside the academic world who deal in ideas, whether they are journalists or freelance writers. Moreover, the definition may be narrowed down by saying that intellectuals communicate their ideas primarily through the written word.

Some sociologists connect the definition of intellectual to culture. By this standard, painters, sculptors, musicians, novelists, poets—the creators of culture—are included in the definition of intellectual. However, for me, the term intellectual has come to mean something different, not necessarily a creator of culture but one who deals specifically in the realm of ideas. America's greatest painter, Jackson Pollock, although extremely well read in the serious literature of his day, was by no means an intellectual. By contrast, his fellow abstract expressionist, Robert Motherwell, indeed was an intellectual by virtue of his many published articles on the meaning of abstract art. Correspondingly, Ernest Hemingway's great literary contribution has become part of our modernist canon. Yet by no means can Hemingway be considered an intellectual. By contrast, James Baldwin's trenchant essays on civil rights make their author an intellectual as well as a fine novelist. Yet this does not mean that great art—Pollock's poured paintings or Hemingway's portrait of the "lost generation"—does not have a profound ideological impact on the modernist psyche. But neither Pollock nor Hemingway was a *practicing* intellectual speaking out on issues in the hurly-burly of the ideological culture wars of their eras. Their art was their ideas.

There are subdivisions within the category of intellectual. First, there are scholars. Scholarship can be defined as the gathering of new and original data with an important conclusion or the significant reinterpretation of existing data. Scholars are in the business of ideas. There are other intellectuals who deal in ideas, but they are not academics and they do not gather data; that is, conduct scientific research. These intellectuals tend to write in journalistic forums and provide commentary on issues and policies, mostly of a polemical nature, which in many cases is extremely insightful and at times has a major impact on our society. Examples would be the bohemian intellectual Michael Harrington's *The Other America*, which directed federal policy towards poverty in America; Rachel Carson's *Silent Spring*, which made protecting the environment a national cause; and Jane Jacobs's *The Death and Life of American Cities*, which had a profound impact on a changing urban America. All of these books were published in the 1960s, and according to one commentator, the transition of the "public intellectual" to the university campus designated these freelance intellectuals as the "last intellectuals." Although the transition of the intellectual to academia has taken place, it has not signaled an end but a major shift in locus of intellectuals. (Harrington joined the academic ranks in 1972 and continued to write intellectual commentary; I began my polemical writing for intellectual magazines in 1966 but was later mentored into scholarship at approximately the same time Harrington entered academia and at the same college—Queens College in New York City.)

KADUSHIN'S AMERICAN INTELLECTUAL ELITE

The standard study which collected survey data on American intellectual life was Charles Kadushin's *The American Intellectual Elite* (1974). Kadushin boldly listed the thirty-three most influential "journals and magazines read by 90 elite American intellectuals in 1970."[7] (I contributed to six of these periodicals during that period.) He went on to identify by name the "seventy most prestigious contemporary American intellectuals (1970)."[8] Kadushin estimated that there were approximately two hundred intellectuals in America at that time.[9]

There were methodological problems with Kadushin's analysis. For one thing, his definition of intellectual was too broad to include novelists such as Saul Bellow and the editorial gatekeepers of these prestigious journals and magazines. For another, his sample was skewed toward New York intellectuals. Sixty percent of his intellectuals lived in New York City. Half of his academics who wrote for these journals were from four universities, two of them Columbia and New York University.[10]

Kadushin's criteria for most important and influential was how often his seventy top intellectuals were published in his sample of thirty-three journals. For example, Irving Howe, whose main influence was as editor of the socialist journal *Dissent*, ranked in the top ten of Kadushin's most important, whereas Howe's socialist colleague Michael Harrington ranked in the twenty-one to twenty-five range. The bottom line is that Harrington redirected national policy with his book on poverty and had a fine biography written about him and an equally great book on his ideological contribution. On the other hand, Howe, initially a literary scholar, influenced few with his polemical commentary. There is little likelihood of his ever being the subject of a biography. The key variable should not have been how often one intellectual appeared in those journals but rather the influence of that person's ideas.

Kadushin's elite intellectuals were squarely on the political left, "more liberal on any issue of public policy than the American public at large, more liberal than another segment of the American elite."[11] By contrast, the American intellectual elite of the year 2000 was overwhelmingly conservative. The proliferation of conservative think tanks, and books, articles, and appearances on televised talk shows by conservatives, helped to revive a dormant conservatism that achieved victory in 1980 with Ronald Reagan, the most conservative president the United States ever had.

Indeed, as Kadushin was conducting his research, the shift to conservatism had already begun. Prominent New York liberal intellectuals were renouncing their liberalism for a form of "neoconservatism." One of their chief neoconservative publications was *The Public Interest*, founded in 1965 by the two prominent neoconservatives and New York intellectuals Irving Kristol and Nathan Glazer. Marilyn Gittell and I were among the first to critique the burgeoning neoconservatism in 1970 in the maiden issue of a New Leftist journal, *Social Policy*. Our piece was titled "In Whose Interest Is the 'Public Interest'?" Glazer responded to the article in the pages of *Commentary*, which under the editorship of Norman Podhoretz was becoming the other major journal of neoconservatism. Kadushin was to publish some of his work in *The Public Interest*.

A polarizing event for the New York intellectuals took place in New York in 1968. The New York City teachers strike over black community control of schools proved to be the watershed moment for the New York intellectuals. Kadushin would classify the Vietnam War and the teachers strikes as "the key symbolic events of the sixties, but in many ways the New York intellectual was more affected by the teachers strike."[12] A mostly Jewish teaching staff led by teachers union leader Albert Shanker sought to dislodge burgeoning black power in elected school boards in three experimental districts. The strike pitted liberal unionists against black and white civil rights activists. There was divisiveness and the high feelings evoked among New York intellectuals who were over-represented by liberal Jews and radicals. (I was heavily involved in the community control movement in an activist think tank and published a reader on the controversy with Marilyn Gittell. We balanced each article pro and con, but in truth, in the intellectual journals, the ratio was three articles in favor of community control to one against.)

Kadushin's analysis has also proved to be outdated. Kadushin anticipated the changing influence of some of his "influential" journals. For example, *The New York Review of Books*, which he named as the number-one magazine in importance, no longer carries the clout it once had. There has been an important shift in venues for ideas. For example, the op-ed pages of national newspapers, such as the *New York Times* and the *Washington Post*, have been established (many mid-sized city newspapers have also adopted the op-ed format to convey ideas on current topics).

Also, the rise of the think tanks separate from academia has created scholars who produce published research with a clear policy bent. Moreover, another important index of influence has been the citation index in libraries begun in 1974: the social science citation index and the humanities index. These count the number of references to a scholar's work in other scholars' works. The importance and influence of a scholar is often measured by the number of citations of his/her work in these indexes.

As a case in point, let us look at the social science citations of Irving Howe in Kadushin's schemata, ranking him in the top ten intellectuals and Michael Harrington in the twenty-one to twenty-five range. The SSCI covers scholarly publications and general intellectual publications, such as those thirty-three journals and magazines named in Kadushin's list of most influential. In the 1975–80 period, the last politically liberal period in America before the Reagan revolution, Michael Harrington was cited over Irving Howe by a substantial margin. By the end of the twentieth century, the citation for Harrington doubled that of Howe despite the fact that Howe's major work, *World of Our Fathers* about the Jewish immigrants, was published in 1976 and Harrington's signature work, *The Other America*, was published a decade and a half earlier, in 1962.

The migration of intellectuals to academia, begun in full force in the 1970s, has given a geographic diversity to the intellectuals in America. No longer can one find the coterie of intellectuals in New York City. Many of the New York intellectuals were Jewish sons and daughters of poor immigrants who were afforded the opportunity to attend a free city college. They had inherited the Marxism and trade unionism of their immigrant parents and proceeded to analyze national and world events through a radical prism. Many kept the faith, but others became true believers of the right.

JACOBY'S "LAST INTELLECTUALS"

One critic of higher education bemoaned the decline—and deaths—of New York intellectuals with his own spiritual Kaddish. Russell Jacoby in *The Last Intellectuals* (1987) scored the extremely few "intellectuals" under the age of thirty-five, even forty-five "as constituting an intellectual generation that . . . simply never appeared."[13] Using Kadushin's dated research as a guide, Jacoby defined intellectuals as "public intellectuals, writers and thinkers who address a general and educated audience."[14] He attributed the disappearance of public intellectuals to the change in American universities with an increase in research demands on faculty. "Younger intellectuals no longer need or want a larger public," he noted.[15] They were too busy pursuing the research within their specialized fields to advance their careers in terms of tenure, promotion, and salary. "Academics write for professional journals that," he wrote, "are unlike the little magazines, creating insular societies."[16] Moreover, Jacoby charged that "independent intellectuals, who wrote for the educated reader, are dying out."[17]

Up to this point, Jacoby is on firm ground. There has been a paradigm shift, not so much among the journals and magazines for the literate general public but in academia. As if to prove Jacoby's point, consider Stanley Fish, a leading professor of English, who defines a public intellectual as "someone to whom the public regularly looks for illumination on any number of (indeed all) issues."[18] By that standard, Fish maintains that "academics are not trained to speak on everything."[19] They may speak on single issues within their expertise, what Fish regards as "rent for a day" intellectuals or "cameo intellectuals," but they are not generalists such as were common among the New York intellectuals.[20] Yet Fish remembers when academics "once did have a pulpit," college presidents who "for a long time carried with them the not only the possibility but the obligation of addressing issues of public concern."[21] College presidents such as James B. Conant of Harvard, Clark Kerr of the University of California, and Robert M. Hutchins of Chicago, as well as others, "cut striking figures on the public stage."[22] But because of fear of offending potential donors in fund-raising efforts, college presidents now remain silent on the great issues of the day. Yet it is precisely because college presidents are silent that more and more faculty fill the void and speak out on issues.

THE RISE OF THE BLACK INTELLECTUALS

While Jacoby and other critics lamented the passing of the New York intellectuals, a new class of intellectuals, beneficiaries of the civil rights movement, rose up. These were the new black intellectuals. There had always been a scattering of black intellectuals, but as a group they did not make themselves felt as forcefully as they did in the 1990s. The organizing principle was not the Marxism of the New York intellectuals, but black nationalism. They were public intellectuals—and they were black. "Like the New York intellectuals," Michael Bérubé wrote in *The New Yorker*, announcing the group's birth, "the new black intellectuals are, to varying degrees, public figures, and, like the New York intellectuals, they seek to redefine what it means to be an intellectual in the United States."[23]

Perhaps the key example is Henry Louis Gates, Jr., of Harvard, who spoke on all manner of black issues in the pages of *The New Yorker*. Gates assembled a talented array of black public intellectuals at Harvard's African American Institute that includes the theologian Cornel West and the sociologist William Julius Wilson. These black intellectuals seek to capture the soul of America. They are not urging, as the New York in-

tellectuals implied, revolution in the streets as practiced by their forebears, the leaders of the civil rights movement. No marching, picketing,
or boycotting. The new black intellectuals are involved in a new form of
politics—"cultural politics," which, as Bérubé notes, "is a kind of com-
pensation for practical politics—more satisfying, more supple, more sus-
ceptible to sheer intellectual virtuosity, because it involves neither
revenues nor statutes."[24] The new intellectual is also, for the most part,
tenured at an elite American university.

Another analysis of "the new intellectuals" defined the public intellectual as "a writer, informed by a strong moral impulse, who addressed a
general, educated audience in accessible language about the most important issues of the day."[25] Robert Boynton describes the New York
intellectuals as "literary curiosities in the museum of culture" who are
now "largely ignored or out of print."[26] In their stead, Boynton describes
a well-formed coterie of black intellectuals who address a new set of
issues that were formed by the civil rights movement, "the defining
event of their lives."[27] "Black intellectuals are important," Boynton
writes, "because they provide a viable, if radically different, image of
what a public intellectual can be."[28]

THE POSTMODERN INTELLECTUAL

Postmodernism has defied precise definition. One of the chief theorists
of postmodernism, Fredric Jameson, would write that "postmodernism
is not widely accepted or even understood today."[29] Postmodernism is
best described as the movement in art, literature, music, and architecture
that emphasized the study of low or popular culture. Postmodernism
rejected the high culture of modernism with its search for the sublime.
This can be illustrated by comparing the spiritual paintings of Mark
Rothko and Jackson Pollock to those of Andy Warhol and Roy Lichten-
stein, which deride popular culture—from conceiving deeply felt ab-
stractions to illustrating cartoons. "Modernism aspired to the sublime,"
Jameson comments.[30]

Jameson best describes the revolt against modernism in these terms:

Those formerly subversive and embattled styles—Abstract Expressionism; The
great modernist poetry of Pound, Eliot or Wallace Stevens; the International Style
(Le Corbusier, Gropius, Mies Van der Roche); Stavinsky; Joyce, Proust and
Mann—felt to be scandalous and shocking by our grandparents are, for the generation which arrives at the gate in the 1960's, felt to be the establishment and
the enemy—dead, stifling, canonical, the reified monuments one has to destroy
to do anything new.[31]

Jameson would describe "the crucial turn" when modernism evolved
into postmodernism as "the 1960's . . . in many ways the key transitional

period."[32] The 1960s were an intensely political period when New Leftists would declare that "the personal is political."[33] The civil rights movement was to give way to the postmodern style of identity politics; from the policy-oriented advocacy of the New York intellectuals to the cultural politics of the black intellectuals.

The political 1960s was also the naissance of the "end of art" theories with the arrival of postmodernism. The Hegelian concept of the "end of history" was reintroduced in the 1980s. Jameson contends that "history does go on," but he solves his postmodern conundrum by adopting Marx's proposition that it is "not the end of history, but the end of prehistory."[34] And with Jameson we not only get an astute narrative of postmodernism, but the founding of cultural studies. Jameson makes connections with cultural, historical, political, economic and philosophical narratives with a tilt to race and gender as variables; in short, the stew that is now called cultural studies. Cultural politics, the new style worn by the postmodern intellectual, emerges from the placenta of cultural studies.

Michael Bérubé touches on the essential difference between the modernist and postmodern intellectual in the chasm between "practical politics" and "cultural politics." He believes in the power of cultural politics to change the hearts and minds of literate America. "When cultural studies engages with the popular and the 'ordinary,' " he writes, "it does so primarily in order to understand—and thereby *change*—the power relations that shape the most intimate and/or quotidian details of our lives."[35]

Bérubé's solution to the problem is to have cultural intellectuals seek the widest audience possible. Bérubé's admonition for literary theorists to become public intellectuals is in response to the conservative public's critique of the influence of the French deconstructionists on literary theory, such as Jacques Derrida and Michel Foucault. Bérubé cites the example of the black intellectuals whose books are prominently displayed—and sold—in bookstores around the country. Yet many of these black authors—though primarily addressing a white audience—have been bought by a rising black middle class. The old-line (modernist) public intellectuals were not interested in the *foule*; they primarily wrote for a power elite, a "happy few," and published in small intellectual journals of opinion. Michael Harrington told intimates that he expected small sales from his classic *The Other America*, but he hoped that the book would be read by decision-makers.

A modernist public intellectual ridiculed the cultural intellectual as "marching on the English Department while the Right took the White House."[36] Todd Gitlin, who had been a member of Students for a Democratic Society in the 1960s, bemoaned the development of "culture as surrogate politics" and the "campus as surrogate world."[37] Gitlin had seen the civil rights movement and the anti-Vietnam War movement transformed in the 1980s into campus culture wars about what and who were to be taught in universities. Although recognizing Michael Bérubé as "a prominent radical professor of English," Gitlin scored the French influence of the deconstructionists so that "the personal was, in short, political—perhaps so much so as to be nothing but political."[38]

Yet Gitlin misses the point. Culture is political. In lieu of street movements, the battle has correctly been raised to a higher and more lasting level: the transformation of the individual. In his concluding essay in *The New Yorker* on black intellectuals, Michael Bérubé hopes for a joining of practical and cultural politics. He admonishes black intellectuals by estimating that they "will have a significant influence on the American political agenda when, and only when, a national party runs on the slogan 'the social justice, stupid'."[39]

Another observer of public intellectuals is Professor John Michael. He analyzes the shift in his study *Anxious Intellectuals: Academic Professionals, Public Intellectuals, and Enlightenment Values* (2000). Michael acknowledges that "the university has become the base of operations" for public intellectuals.[40] He finds that "the real problem" of these campus intellectuals is "what roles do they feel themselves capable of playing in contemporary society" within the matrix of the American university?[41]

Perhaps we can grasp more fully the differences between the modernist public intellectual and the postmodern one by offering profiles of prime examples of each. Both Michael Harrington, the consummate modernist, and Henry Louis Gates, Jr., the classic postmodernist, have much to tell us about the differences between the two styles. Michael Harrington was a typical bohemian intellectual living in the Greenwich Village of the 1950s. He did most of his best work as a freelancer before joining academia, without a doctorate, to teach at Queens College in New York City at the age of forty-five. Henry Louis Gates, Jr., began in academia and later headed the African American Institute at Harvard University.

Harrington, from the Midwest, was born in 1928, the son of an affluent bourgeois family. He went east to attend a Jesuit university. His father was a patent attorney, his mother a teacher. Harrington graduated from Holy Cross College and attended Yale Law School for one year before he decided that writing was to be his career. He became a member of the pacifist radical Catholic Worker group in New York City for two years before renouncing his faith and becoming a life long Socialist. He found the personalism of the worker too constricting. Living in the Village, Harrington freelanced as staff member for a study of the blacklist commissioned by the liberal Fund for the Republic. He first appeared in print at the young age of 23 with a piece in the prestigious journal *Partisan Review*, home of the New York intellectuals. He was a decade younger than most of the New York intellectuals and he was not Jewish, but he could very well be considered part of that group.

Harrington was a regular contributor to the leading liberal/leftist journals of that era: *Partisan Review, Commentary, Commonweal, Village Voice,* and *Dissent.* He eventually wrote a column on social issues for the *New York Herald Tribune.* His clear and cogent presentation of ideas won him the respect of many of his adversaries, and he appeared on William Buckley's *Firing Line* program many times before his death at age sixty-one in 1989.

In his first memoir, *Fragments of a Century,* Harrington described his decade-long bohemian routine of reading and writing during the day and drinking at the White Horse Tavern in Greenwich Village at night. "You could see me, punctually dissolute," he wrote, "appear on week nights at midnight and on weekends at one o'clock."[42] Later, after marriage and the advent of two children, Harrington sought stability in a post in academia, ostensibly for health care for his family.

It was one book, the product of a piece in *Commentary* entitled "Our Fifty Million Poor" written in 1959, that would establish his credentials as a mainstream public intellectual. The book was *The Other America,* an impassioned declaration that large-scale poverty existed and that government had the power to abolish poverty. *The Other America* struck a nerve in an affluent America. It was read by President John Kennedy, and it jump-started the federal government's poverty program initiated by Kennedy's successor Lyndon Johnson. *The Other America* was the classic example of speaking truth to power. The book was published at an opportune moment, when the federal government began relying on social science research to develop long-term policies.

I was acquainted with Harrington, first meeting him in the late 1950s when I was a young Catholic labor radical (the Association of Catholic Trade Unionists that emerged from the Catholic Worker movement). I joined the Socialist Party in the 1960s. Harrington assembled two dozen intellectuals and labor radicals, and I was included, for a monthly salon to discuss social policy. Most important, I was one of the first reviewers of *The Other America* for *Kirkus Reviews,* a prepublication reviewing agency targeted to libraries. Mine was the only ambivalent review he received among his many praises. It is a review I wish now that I could rewrite.

Harrington wrote sixteen books and hundreds of articles, and appeared frequently on public radio and television to champion his ideas. His aim was always to convert the decision-makers rather than convert the multitude. It was the example of the Jesuits who tried to make China a Catholic nation by concentrating on converting the mandarins. In short, once the policymakers are won over, change results; and the masses will follow.

The majority of Harrington's books sought to change America into a more compassionate welfare state. The titles of some of these indicate his direction: *Towards a Democratic Left, The New American Poverty, The Vast Majority, Decade of Decision, The Next America Socialism: Past and Present, The Twilight of Capitalism*. Only one book could qualify in the cultural studies genre, *The Politics at God's Funeral*, which was a philosophical treatise of a better world not based on religious belief.

The activism of the Catholic Worker seemed merely, in the words of Harrington, the "politics of the moral gesture."[43] He preferred the intellectualism of the Socialists. Harrington spent his first ten years in the Socialist Party under the monitorship of the legendary Trotskyite Max Schactman, and went on to publish dozens of essays before his first book appeared.

With the publication of *The Other America*, his second book, Harrington had learned, in his words, how to "speak American." His lifelong ambition was to create a democratic socialist movement that would be distinctly American. In that respect, he failed. But, in one manner or another, he influenced a generation of thinkers who have carried on the torch of social reform. Both Cornel West and William Julius Wilson, for example, credit Harrington with giving them the intellectual framework for their analyses of social issues.

Harrington had not expected the success that came with the publication of *The Other America*. Living in bohemian poverty in the Village, he had hoped that sales would exceed 2,500 copies and that his book would receive respectful reviews. When President Kennedy read the book and established it as a cornerstone for his social programs, Harrington's fame and financial success were secured. In addition to becoming a consultant to two presidents, Harrington served as an advisor to Martin Luther King, Jr. Eventually his reputation traversed the Atlantic, and he became America's best-known Socialist. Harrington was also something of a media celebrity.

This enormous early success (Harrington was only thirty-two when *The Other America* was published) resulted in a nervous breakdown. I recall greeting Harrington in Union Square during that period, and seeing him jump away out of fear. Still, he was able to write and lecture during this difficult period.

The cultural revolution of the 1960s, however, pushed Harrington and other Socialists to the sidelines. He opposed the New Left Students for a Democratic Society because of their softness on communism, and he was instrumental in expelling SDS from a wing of the Socialist Party. (He later came to regret his role in the expulsion.)

Harrington also waffled in his opposition to the Vietnam War and devoted more time to criticizing far-left opponents than to criticizing war supporters. And he became uncomfortable with the civil rights movement after it shifted its focus from integration to Black Power. Indeed, Harrington's critique of the black community control movement in schools—the first fleshing out of Black Power—alienated him from emerging black leaders. It also resulted in a rift between Harrington and other white intellectuals. Having been involved in the black community control movement myself, I felt compelled to resign from the Socialist Party when I found myself in opposition to Harrington's position.

By the early 1970s, Harrington's influence had waned. Factionalism within the Socialist Party resulted in a split, and membership declined. Increasingly, Harrington was perceived by most Americans as a mainstream liberal. He sought consolation in ties with European democratic socialists.

Culturally, Harrington was a Europhile. He admired the work of thinkers whose roots were European: Marx, of course, but especially scholars of action such as André Malraux. At Harrington's deathbed was a copy of E.M. Forster's *Howards End*. Harrington made annual pilgrimages to France and was delighted to be able to speak French to one of his doctors in his final days. The irony was that this most American of American Socialists had the picture on the cover of his biography by Maurice Isserman, *The Other American*, facing the cathedral of Notre Dame in Paris. The picture was selected by Harrington's wife.

Still, the American media took note when Harrington died in 1989. Most of the praise, of course, focused on the impact of *The Other America*. And perhaps that's understandable. Of his sixteen books, only a few still have power. One might say that he peaked with his seminal work on American poverty.

Henry Louis Gates Jr. has been anointed by literate America as the black public intellectual. From his position as chairperson of Harvard University's African American Studies Institute and his regular essays in *The New Yorker*, Gates has wielded enormous cultural influence. One journalist has called Gates the "head Negro in charge" who is no less than "the most influential black man in the United States today."[44]

This estimate of Gates is echoed by the mainstream press. *Time* magazine identified him in 1997 as one of its "25 most influential Americans"; *Newsweek* listed him as "100 Americans to watch for in the next century"; and the *New York Times* has called him the top "academodstar."[45] He has received the MacArthur "genius" award and the American Book Award for his book *The Signifying Monkey*.

Gates is the quintessential postmodern intellectual. A professor of English, he has broadened out to become a major black public intellectual. He is the author of *The Signifying Monkey: A Theory of Afro-American Literary Criticism* (1988), which is a deconstruction of black literary texts. He has entered the culture wars with his book *Loose Canons: Notes on the Culture Wars* (1992).

But his main aim is for black cultural identity. Gates has written a memoir of growing up black, *Colored People* (1994), and followed that with books plumbing the African American experience and heritage: *The Norton Anthology of African-American Literature* (1996), *Thirteen Ways of Looking at a Black Man* (1977), and with Cornel West *The Future of The Race* (1996). In addition, Gates produced for the BBC and PBS a televised documentary on Africa.

Gates was born in 1950 in Piedmont, West Virginia, to parents who were working poor. His father had two jobs—loading trucks at the paper mill and working nights as a janitor for the phone company. His mother worked cleaning the houses of whites. Gates was a "confessed mama's boy," and when he grew up he was shocked to know "how deeply my mother despised white people."[46] The irony was that Gates would marry a white woman.

Gates was precocious at school and first attended Potomac State College. He then transferred to Yale University where he graduated as a history major summa cum laude. He completed his doctoral work in English at Cambridge University. His first intellectual stirrings of ethnic awareness came with reading James Baldwin's *Notes of a Native Son*, calling it a "voice capturing the terrible exhilaration and anxiety of being a person of African descent in this country."[47] Gates spent his junior year in Tanzania, the first of many trips to Africa. In Africa, the "main thing" he learned "was how American I am."[48]

One of his major influences was W.E.B. DuBois. Gates subscribed to DuBois's call for a "talented tenth" of the black intelligentsia to lead the African American community. DuBois wrote that "the Negro race, like all races is going to be saved by its exceptional men, who will comprise 'a Talented Tenth'."[49] Gates wrote of DuBois that "he became the second great African-American public intellectual" after Frederick Douglas.[50] He said that DuBois was to "narrate a black dual nationhood: a nationality at once American yet paradoxically and resonantly African-American."[51] Yet, Gates did not subscribe to DuBois's Marxism. "There's not going to be a socialist revolution," Gates told an interviewer, "O.K. how do you humanize capitalism?"[52] Gates would create a W.E.B DuBois Institute at Harvard for research on African American issues.

Gates taught at a number of elite universities before settling in 1991 at Harvard University to revive the university's African American Studies Institute. He launched from that position a stellar cast—from the "talented tenth"—to wage cultural war on the majoritarian society. He recruited such academic talent as Cornel West, theologian and social analyst from Princeton, and William Julius Wilson, sociologist and policy analyst from the University of Chicago, among others. Both West and Wilson are members of the Democratic Socialists of America, Michael Harrington's loosely organized group. Wilson wrote a blurb for Michael

Harrington's *The New American Poverty* and Harrington wrote one for Wilson's *The Truly Disadvantaged*.

Despite West and Wilson's policy orientation, Gates concerns himself with culture, and a postmodern culture. He was described by a journalist as a professor who "delights in popular culture."[53] One indication of his orientation is that he teaches one of his two yearly courses at Harvard on autobiography and memoir of African Americans. His buzzword is "narrative," whereas West and Wilson's is "policy." As an example, in 1990 Gates testified on behalf of a black rap group, 2 Live Crew, in their trial on obscenity. He has been quoted as saying that "if Jesse Jackson kept his nose out of literary criticism, he would let him speak in the political realm."[54]

His strongest criticism has come from the left wing of the black community. Professor Adolph Reed, Jr., calls Gates "a freelance advocate for black centrism."[55] And an activist black minister, Reverend Eugene F. Rivers, Jr., has called Gates's cultural politics a "let-them-eat literature" approach that neglects an activist research agenda.[56]

CONCLUSION

A number of questions remain unresolved about the role of the public intellectual. How supportive are universities concerning their public intellectuals? Is cultural politics alone, rooted in a postmodern low culture sufficient to influence the progress of a developed society?

Cultural politics often translates into identity politics—emphasizing race and gender—rather than a politics based on class issues. That can prove deadly for African Americans who comprise only 12 percent of the population and Latinos who hover around 9 percent of the population. It can be a strategy resembling an embattled circle around the wagon train. Indeed, when one analyzes the policy shifts of the last twenty years, minorities have seen a slow erosion in the gains established by the Kennedy-Johnson New Frontier and Great Society. Now more than ever, a coalition politics—Jesse Jackson's Rainbow Coalition of blacks, Latinos and whites—is needed. When the civil rights leader Bayard Rustin argued in his 1965 piece in *Commentary* "From Protest To Politics" for maintaining the Rooseveltian coalition, his pleas fell on deaf ears. Rustin was out of step with the Black Power movement, which emphasized controlling ghetto institutions and black pride. With thirty-five years of tripling of the black middle class through affirmative action and the substantive election of black politicians to office, coalition politics deserves another look.

However, the biggest civil rights action is hip-hop music with its angry social cry. A few years ago Jesse Jackson was challenged by an angry high school student at an assembly where he spoke. "Mr. Jackson," the student charged, "you're 1964, I'm 1998." Certainly, the politics of 1964 without the cultural politics of the present will not succeed. But so far they have operated on parallel tracks and not converged. The role of the intellectual who has moved beyond modernism and postmodernism is to help create a viable past and a viable politics that are beyond modernist and postmodernist sensibilities.

NOTES

1. Gail Sheehy, *Character: America's Search for Leadership* (New York: William Morrow and Co., 1988), p. 160.

2. Richard Hofstadter, *Anti-Intellectualism in American Life* (New York: Knopf, 1963), p. 407.

3. Ibid.

4. Bob Herbert, "In America," *New York Times*, August 28, 2000, p. A21.

5. *New Yorker*, July 31, 2000, pp. 56–57.

6. *New York Times* Sunday Magazine, December 15, 1996, pp. 48–49.

7. Charles Kadushin, *The American Intellectual Elite* (New York: Basic Books, 1974), p. 41.

8. Ibid., p. 30.

9. Ibid., p. 19.

10. Ibid., pp. 22–23.

11. Ibid., p. 27.

12. Ibid., p. 78.

13. Russell Jacoby, *The Last Intellectuals: American Culture in the Age of Academe* (New York: Basic Books, 1987), p. 3.

14. Ibid., p. 5.

15. Ibid., p. 6.

16. Ibid., p. 7.

17. Ibid.

18. Stanley Fish, *Professional Correctness: Literary Studies and Political Change* (Oxford, England: Clarendon Press, 1995), p. 119.

19. Ibid.

20. Ibid., p. 18

21. Ibid.

22. Ibid., p. 120.

23. Michael Bérubé, "Public Academy," *New Yorker*, January 15, 1995, p. 75.

24. Ibid., p. 79.

25. Robert Boynton, "The New Intellectuals," *Atlantic Monthly*, March, 1995, p. 53.

26. Ibid., p. 54.

27. Ibid., p. 61.

28. Ibid., p. 28.

29. Fredric Jameson, *The Crucial Turn: Selected Writing on the Postmodern 1983–1998* (London: Verso, 1998), p. 1.

30. Ibid., p. 83.

31. Ibid., p. 2.

32. Ibid., p. 3.

33. Maurice Isserman, *The Other American: The Life of Michael Harrington* (New York: Public Affairs Press, 2000), p. 34.

34. Jameson, *The Crucial Turn*, p. 88.

35. Michael Bérubé, "Public Academy," p. 40.

36. Todd Gitlin, *The Twilight of Common Dreams: Why America is Wracked by Culture Wars* (New York: Metropolitan Books, 1995), p. 125.

37. Ibid., p. 151.

38. Ibid., pp. 95, 152.

39. Michael Bérubé, "Public Academy," p. 40.

40. John Michael, *Anxious Intellectuals: Academic Professionals, Public Intellectuals, and Enlightenment Values* (Durham, North Carolina: Duke University Press, 2000), p. 171.

41. Ibid.

42. Michael Harrington, *Fragments of a Century* (New York: Saturday Review Press, 1973), p. 48.

43. Isserman, *The Other American*, p. 230.

44. Cheryl Bentsen, "Head Negro in Charge," *Boston Magazine*, 1990, p. 1.

45. Ibid., p. 2.

46. Brian Lamb, "Interview with Henry Louis Gates, Jr.," *Booknotes*, October 9, 1994 (C-SPAN Television Transcript), p. 5.

47. Ibid., p. 5.

48. Ibid., p. 6.

49. Ibid., p. 8.

50. W.E.B. DuBois, "The Talented Tenth," in Henry Louis Gates, Jr., and Cornel West, *The Future of the Race* (New York: Vintage Books, 1996), p. 159.

51. Ibid., p. 116.

52. Jane Slaughter, "Interview with Henry Louis Gates, Jr.," *Progressive*, January, 1998, p. 3.

53. Cheryl Bentsen, "Head Negro in Charge," p. 13.

54. Jane Slaughter, "Interview with Henry Louis Gates, Jr.," p. 2.

55. Ibid., p. 1.

56. Cheryl Bentsen, "Head Negro in Charge," p. 23.

2

The Socially Conscious University

In 1978, my book *The Urban University in America* was published, setting a social agenda for urban universities. I observed that urban universities were more than temples of learning. Urban universities were players in the city: They had an economic impact with their payrolls, and they served to train city workers by teaching government and social work. In some cities such as Boston, urban universities constituted the main industry. In short, urban universities were more than ivory towers.

Consequently, I suggested that these universities had a moral responsibility toward their urban communities. "An urban university," I wrote, "should be an institution developed specially for the purpose of relating to the wide range of issues faced by cities and their communities."[1] This quote is used in a brochure for Northeastern University which states that, "for a hundred years, Northeastern University has been closely connected to the economic, social and cultural life of metropolitan Boston."[2]

Not everyone agreed with the "shoulds" in my book. Harold Enarson, then president of Ohio University, reviewing *The Urban University* for the *Journal of Higher Education*, thought me naïve. "The central difficulty in this provocative book," he wrote, "is that the author loads upon a new imagined federal grant urban university all the reforms he wishes for American high education."[3] In this chapter, I shall revisit those suggested reforms while examining all of higher education from that social prism.

UNIVERSITIES UNDER ATTACK

For the past decade there has been a concerted attack to dumb down America's universities. This is in spite of the fact that the American university system, especially because of its graduate schools, is generally regarded as the best in the world.

Why has this happened? The reason for this criticism of American universities has been to reinforce teaching, which allegedly has suffered from an excessive emphasis on research by professors. But one hidden motivation is to intimidate faculty members who are perceived, according to several polls, as being overwhelmingly politically liberal. In a largely conservative nation, universities are perceived as the hotbeds of a dangerous liberalism.

Who are the critics? They are mostly journalists and conservative politicians who have difficulty understanding the nature of higher education and the process of learning. Syndicated columnist Matthew Miller recommends that there should be a "cracking down on dubious research" that is essentially "idle, tenure-earning junk with little or no social value."[4] The result, according to Miller, would be that "you could shed 100,000 of today's 550,000 full-time professors without students noticing," since a faculty member typically spends a quarter of his/her time on research.[5]

Miller repeats a common misunderstanding about higher education. The elemental truth is that, without research, there would be no content. If a professor is not pursuing research, he or she is not on the cutting edge of the thinking in his or her area of expertise. Most journalists, and most of the public, do not comprehend the scholarly process. That is partly the fault of the many professors who make little attempt to communicate to the public what they do. For example, most scholarly books with new data and new interpretations (including mine) have a shelf life of a few short years before another scholar adds to the body of knowledge.

In the past thirty years, the explosion of knowledge in all areas has been enormous. Consequently, textbooks that are based on others' research are out of date as soon as they are published. Only when a professor pursues research is there effective teaching.

John Dewey, one of the world's great philosophers and the father of modern educational philosophy, wrote forty books and 700 articles. By today's standards, he would be classified as a disastrous teacher. Dewey's problem was that he lacked charisma in the classroom. He would sit down during class, stare out the window, and drone on in a boring voice. Many of Dewey's students thought him a dreadful teacher; his best students found him to be a moral force. I would have given anything to have been exposed to his genius. However, in today's academic milieu, Dewey might have had a difficult time obtaining tenure.

Literary theory has become the chief whipping boy of the critics of higher education. Feminist scholars have offered a new way of looking at literary figures, known as "queer theory." It is an unfortunate name for a profound idea.

Queer theory merely states that the genders of literary figures may be interchangeable, that a character in a novel or a play who was written as a man may have the attributes of a woman and vice versa, thus further expanding the notion of gender.

Queer theory has enabled me to take a fresh look at classic literary figures. For example, I now find that after a lifetime of identifying with Rhett Butler in *Gone with the Wind*, I have more in common with Scarlett O'Hara. Scarlett possesses more of the traditionally "manly" assertive traits associated with leadership than anyone else in the novel. Indeed, Scarlett has more going for her than do most military generals.

Is queer theory "dubious research"? I think not.

Is there such a thing as "dubious research"? My answer is that all research by its very nature advances the body of knowledge, and thus is necessary. Yet in my field of education, there has been an agonizing reappraisal of the "awful reputation of educational research," as one scholar has put it.

Educational research was challenged more than a decade ago by Chester E. Finn, Jr., then assistant secretary for research in President Ronald Reagan's Department of Education. For Finn, educational research "had not fulfilled its role in the effort to improve our schools."[6] Most educational scholars found Finn's definition of research too constricting.

We owe our students the most broadening intellectual experience possible. The search for knowledge—research—imparts to students the importance of developing the human intellect to its outermost limits. Perhaps the final words belong to John Dewey: "Every thinker puts some portion of an apparently stable world in peril, and no one can wholly predict what will emerge in its place."[7]

The attack on universities has come from the conservative right, but it has enjoyed much public support in the media. These critics argue that universities have lowered standards (Allan Bloom, *The Closing of the American Mind*, 1987); that universities have been captured by an elitist leftist professoriate (Dinesh D'Souza, *Illiberal Education*, 1991; Roger Kimball, *Tenured Radicals*, 1990; and Russell Jacoby, *Dogmatic Wisdom*, 1995); and that professors were underworked and overpaid and largely responsible for the deteriorating condition of American colleges and universities (Charles Sykes, *ProfScam*, 1988). These books became bestsellers.

The counterattack came from the left. Such books as Michael Bérubé's

Public Access (1994), Stanley Fish's *Professional Correctness* (1995), Lawrence Levine's *The Opening of the American Mind* (1995), and Gerald Graff's *Beyond the Culture Wars* (1995) responded by positing a resilient university that revised its literary canon and was still developing as a cultural institution. These books did not become best-sellers. The conservatives won the culture wars in the media and in the bookstores. The educational liberals and leftists won the war on the college campuses.

A more moderate defense of higher education was made by Harvard Dean of Arts and Sciences Henry Rosovsky. In *The University: An Owner's Manual* (1990), Rosovsky paints a bland, calm picture of what a university does. He posits as "the purpose of liberal education" that "an educated person must be able to think," that "an educated person should have . . . an informed acquaintance . . . with the sciences" and be aware of the "scholarly, literary, and artistic achievement of the past" and "with the major religious and philosophical conceptions of mankind."[8]

Moreover, Rosovsky offered a more tempered version of research. "In general, the university social contracts," he writes, "almost always unwritten—is well understood: professors in universities are expected to spend half their time in teacher-related activities and half their time in research-related activities . . . to be a producer of new knowledge."[9]

UNIVERSITY PRESIDENTS AS "MORAL LEADERS"

For the past fifty years American college and university presidents have developed a cautious persona regarding large social issues. They have become a silent generation of higher education leaders.

Part of the reason is that the main function of university presidents has changed. They have essentially become fund-raisers whose main job is to obtain money from wealthy alumni if they head private institutions, or from the state if they are in charge of public institutions. Consequently, more and more university presidents are urged to follow a corporate business style of management. They tend to be consumed by an edifice complex in expanding their universities. Commentary on social issues jeopardizes the fragile relationship with respective alumni or legislators when it comes time to obtain necessary funding.

Now that role of "public intellectual" has fallen, almost by default, on university faculty. A handful of professors serve as the academic conscience of America. They write for newspapers and intellectual magazines, and they appear on television and radio using their expertise as scholars to comment on contemporary issues.

But they do so at a price. Some university administrators—and many professors—do not view the public intellectual's work as important and do not reward it in terms of tenure, promotion, or salary. They see it as a departure from scholarship, although actually there are few public intellectuals who are not productive scholars. However, public intellectuals feel that they can speak out on issues of the body of research they have conducted as scholars.

Sometimes a chilling effect occurs when a professor writes a critical analysis of a policy. City officials and legislators may complain to university presidents about the lack of support by the university for a special project. University presidents are then confronted with the need to preserve academic freedom, while doing enough damage control to ensure harmonious relations with potential sources of money.

Moreover, at some institutions professors are not encouraged to speak out on sensitive topics in the community. The bottom line is that both professors and university presidents have more responsibility to exert a role as public intellectuals. As John Dewey pointed out, education is more than intellectual learning; it has a moral aspect as well. The community of scholars has an obligation to society to join in the public dialogue.

A 1994 study by Rita Bornstein, president of Rollins College, accentuated the lack of moral leadership by university presidents. Bornstein argued that "the prestige of the college presidency assures an audience for a president's ideas" but that "college and university presidents are perceived as silent and lacking in leadership on important public policy issues."[10] Her research confirmed that view.

Bornstein surveyed 167 presidents of independent, coeducational, and nondenominational institutions. The presidents were *not* asked about their public role on educational issues. Her data showed that "most presidents" do not become involved in controversial public policy issues or partisan politics for fear of "offending diverse constituencies ... [and having a negative] ... impact on fundraising."[11] Eighty-two percent of presidents surveyed stated that "presidents should subvert their personal views and political beliefs to the interests of their institutions."[12] Nevertheless, Bornstein believes that "college and university presidents have an important role to play in public debate on policy issues."[13]

What is to be done? Bornstein suggests that "the key to liberating a college president to serve society as a public intellectual is the explicit endorsement of that role by trustees and regents."[14] The problem with that solution is that most boards of trustees are culled from the most conservative areas in society—law, finance, and communications. As I pointed on in *The Urban University in America*, universities are "governed mainly by pillars of the middle and upper class Americans, the inheritors of the American way."[15] These board members, "having done well by America, are convinced the system works."[16] I noted in the case of the board of trustees of Columbia University that "none was a poet, writer nor scholar."[17] Nor was any a poor resident from the Harlem community abutting Columbia. Boards of trustees are not representative of American society.

On the one end of the spectrum, we have a manual for college presidents titled *Presidential Leadership* (1996) by James L. Fisher and James V. Koch. The manual neglects to mention the role of public intellectual for college presidents, but it is a practical guide for dealing with politicians, the media, students, and boards of trustees, among other issues. On the other hand, Stephen James Nelson has compiled a useful collection of the exceptions to the rule in his book *Leaders in the Crucible: The Moral Voice of College Presidents* (2000). Nelson notes that "for more than two hundred fifty years from the founding of Harvard to the beginning of the twentieth century, the image of the college president as moral leader persisted and predominated."[18] Now most Americans, according to an American Council on Education study, believe "that college and university presidents are concerned more about their institutions than they are about students and the best interest of the public."[19] A majority of those surveyed by ACE think that when "college presidents speak publicly about issues, their first concern is their institutions."[20]

What has changed structurally about the college president is the evolution from academic-scholar-administrator to corporate chief executive of a large business. In his history of higher education, Christopher J. Lucas notes "the emergence of American Higher education as a corporate enterprise."[21] He writes that colleges and universities have assumed

Much of the trappings of large-scale business organizations: mission statements, strategic planning, elaborate budgeting systems, meticulous record-keeping, cost-effectiveness analysis, marketing research, public relations efforts, total quality management, hierarchical governance structures and pyramidal bureaucracies.[22]

Corporate presidencies have increasingly been filled by academic economists. Rosovsky observed that "the Presidents of Princeton, Northwestern, and Michigan in recent years have all been practitioners of the dismal science."[23] My president at Old Dominion for eleven years, James V. Koch, co-author of *Presidential Leadership*, is an economist.

But there have been calls to reinstitute the "moral voice" of college presidents. One such public intellectual, Reverend Theodore M. Hesburch, in his years at the University of Notre Dame recently bemoaned the silence of University presidents and hoped "that more of our presidents were willing to take the lead in tackling . . . issues."[24]

Stephen James Nelson predicts a pendulum swing from the corporate presidency to "returning to scholar presidents who are likely to be more attuned to the importance of moral leadership."[25]

Perhaps he is right. Two examples might suffice. President George Rupp's commencement address at Columbia in 2000 cited "disparities in income and wealth (that) continue to grow" worldwide.[26] Rupp regarded global poverty as "the most fundamental challenge" of this century.[27] At Harvard's commencement the same year, President Neil Rudenstine focussed on "the value of freedom" worldwide but admonished that "the use of force in human affairs must be far more limited than in earlier eras."[28]

A MODEL ACADEMIC VILLAGE

When I wrote *The Urban University in America*, I noted studies indicating that these universities had reacted with urban renewal policies that impinged on the minority poor. These urban neighborhoods had in many cases deteriorated into slums. The answer seemed to be to take advantage of a federal urban renewal program to remove slums and relocate the poor to other deprived neighborhoods in the city. Ghetto activists saw urban renewal as black removal, and they opposed the universities. The mind-set of Jacques Barzun, then Provost of Columbia University, exemplified that of many university presidents grappling with the problem of universities embedded in slums. "The relationship of students and faculty to the community," Barzun declared, "requires the perpetual *que vive* of the paratrooper in enemy country."[29]

Consequently, confrontations between town and gown took place in cities across America. "The sad fact," I wrote, "has been that the urban university is distrusted in the cities by the encircling poor."[30] I argued for enlightened policies that would play "a beneficial role in creating greater harmony between the university and the city."[31] Since then, some sporadic efforts have been made to ease the town-gown conflict. Yale University has offered to subsidize faculty willing to live in New Haven in order to give the city a more balanced economic mix.

A new paradigm in grappling with the problem of town-gown was struck by the president of Trinity College in Hartford, Connecticut. Evan S. Dobelle established a "grand vision" for university expansion that serves as a model for academic villages in urban America. First, Dobelle's plan calls for buying the homes of the poor, renovating them, and selling them back to the original residents at reduced-rate mortgages. Then, these same residents would be given training for employment opportunities at the college. In addition, three schools would be built for area students that would span elementary to high school and be technologically up to date.

The question for universities is to have university presidents generate the necessary resources to embark on such a bold plan. In one respect, Dobelle has an uncommon advantage over his other presidential colleagues. He is not an academic but a politician who has been mayor of a city and aide to various governors and a senator, among other political affiliations. He has been described as "more slick politician than tweedy academic."[32] Dobelle was able to raise $175 million for his project from city, state, and federal agencies as well as from Hartford institutions, such as hospitals in the renewal area. Federal Housing and Urban Development officials knew of no other plan as imaginative for urban renewal in the United States.

By contrast, consider the "university village" created by my Old Dominion University. Situated in Norfolk, Virginia, home of the largest naval base in the world, the university enrolls 18,000 students. Norfolk is at the hub of four other cities with a total combined population of 1.2 million. Old Dominion is bordered by a middle-class section north of its campus and a poor section to the south and east. A few years back, a white resident student was murdered in a poor section of the city adjacent to the university campus. The president called it the worst event of his many years in higher education.

The response to this crime was swift and sweeping. A huge plan to redevelop the poor neighborhood into a stable academic village was created. The plan called for razing sixty-seven acres of land that featured existing homes for the poor and small businesses into a model campus village with a 10,000-seat convocation center, office facilities, restaurants, and shopping. The master plan called the effort "truly the Village of the 21st Century and a model of national significance."[33] Unfortunately, the academic village is more of the same urban renewal effort that has characterized university expansions in the past. The poor are left out. The Trinity College experiment is truly the model that changes the paradigm.

URBAN STUDIES AND BLACK STUDIES

By the new millennium the surge for urban studies programs and centers had ended, and a reverse process of decline took place. Part of the problem was the shift in national attitudes. Eliminating poverty—a core of urban studies courses—had disappeared as a national goal. William Julius Wilson, the African American sociologist at Harvard, wrote in 1988 that poverty was no longer a national issue for many scholars. Wilson noted that, regarding poverty, "liberals had ignored these problems throughout most of the 1970s."[34]

U.S. presidents failed to mention poverty—and urban issues—in their state-of-the-union messages. Many scholars followed suit by dismissing the problems of poverty. For example, a text used in many introductory urban studies courses, Roger W. Cave's *Exploring Urban America* (1995), which is a collection of articles from the academic journal *Urban Affairs Quarterly*, fails to have either a section or an article solely devoted to the issue of poverty.

In their heyday there were hundreds of urban studies programs and some three hundred urban institutes and centers working on community issues. One counted fifty master's degree programs and eleven doctor's degree programs.[35] By the end of the millennium there existed a mere eighty-two urban studies programs and centers—a precipitous decline.[36] Urban studies was no longer where the action was on college campuses. In many instances, a new developing field closely allied to urban studies arose on campuses: policy studies. A few degree programs emerged under the more encompassing form of policy studies. The Rand Institute, for example, which is unaffiliated with universities, offered a doctorate in policy analysis.

Budget cuts in the 1980s forced many urban centers to close. As a case in point, my university, Old Dominion, initiated a master's degree program in urban studies in 1974. That was followed five years later with a doctorate in urban studies. The faculty of the program operated a successful conference each year—Urban South Conference—that drew hundreds of scholars and students. Moreover, an urban center to address concrete urban problems was opened, funded jointly by area businesses and the university. Fiscal retrenchment in the State of Virginia in the mid-1980s forced the university to eliminate the conference and the urban center.

Black studies initially suffered a fate similar to that of urban studies. At the height of the demand for black studies in 1971, there were some 500 universities with black studies programs. This number declined to 300 programs six years later.[37] A mere half dozen offered master's degrees in the discipline, including Harvard. Harvard's program, in disarray by the 1990s was revived by Henry Louis Gates, Jr., who brought in academic superstars such as William Julius Wilson and Cornel West to make Harvard's program, arguably, the most recognizable of all such programs in the United States.

A number of developments have occurred in the history of black studies. *The Journal of Black Studies* was founded by Molefi Kete Assante in 1971. Assante is one of a host of black scholars—such as Henry Louis Gates, Jr., Cornel West, and William Julius Wilson of Harvard—who have made a fruitful field of African American studies. These scholars have so enriched the field to attract students that, according to the black scholar Manning Marable of Columbia University, "African American studies is experiencing a new wave of popularity."[38] Moreover, Marable points out that "most major universities now recommend as part of their core curricula or distribution requirements a menu of multicultural courses that usually includes black studies."[39]

Most interesting is the metamorphosing of black studies into ethnic studies programs. Modeled on the University of California/Berkeley ethnic studies program are approximately one hundred ethnic studies programs and thirty departments.[40] Berkeley's Department of Ethnic Studies, created in 1969, had four distinct ethnic strands: African American Studies, Chicano Studies, Asian Studies, and Native American Studies. Consequently, with the rise of prominent black and ethnic scholars and the revamping of programs, black and ethnic studies are enjoying a cultural renaissance.

WOMEN'S STUDIES

Feminists credited both the civil rights movement and the New Left in the 1960s with the emergence of the women's movement. "The New Left had a vision of an egalitarian society," Catherine Stimpson wrote, "[and] helped raise a substantial following for the women's movement."[41] She further observed that in the Black Power phase of the civil rights movement, "blacks insisted on courses that looked at the Afro-American experience; women demanded courses on the female experience."[42] Catherine Stimpson noted that "the traditionally conservative nature of scholarship" was undermined by "the highly influential *The Structure of Scientific Revolutions* (1962) by Thomas Kuhn," which "did much to strengthen skepticism over tradition by showing that even the allegedly 'objective' sciences are not value free."[43]

By the 1970s, as both urban and black studies programs and departments declined, there occurred the beginnings of women's studies on college campuses. Women's studies owed a debt to the Black Power phase of the civil rights movement in the late 1960s. Once the goal of civil rights activists became the redemption of a usable past raising the question of who am I? it was but a small step for women to do so. The feminist movement spawned journals such as *Signs*, which were dedicated to the scholarly examination of women's issues. Academic feminist books crossed over to trade books and were much in demand by the general public.

The first women's studies program began at San Diego State University in 1969–70. In 1977, an umbrella organization was formed for the burgeoning programs—the National Women's Studies Association.[44] As of 2001, there are 621 such programs. One hundred and two universities offer graduate work in women studies, and only five institutions offer a master's degree in the discipline. Many of these programs relied on foundation support. By 1986, for example, the Ford Foundation had dispensed $70 million to women's studies throughout the nation. The Ford Foundation funded the beginning of *Signs* in 1975, the first women's issues journal.[45]

A 1998–99 study by NWSA gives a clearer picture of the status of women's studies. A questionnaire was sent to the member institutions, and 187 replied. A clear majority of these (140 of 187) were found to be merely programs. Only 22 had the full stature of departments. Most of the programs (65) were in research/doctoral institutions and most (93–95) were in suburban or rural campuses rather than in urban centers.[46]

Women's studies focuses on the centrality of the feminist perspective. The hope is that students will have their consciousness raised as a result of feminist studies. One report on women's studies claims that "students typically undergo a profound transformation as they claim more knowledge" so that they "pass through an identifiable series of moments of recognition" of their feminist identity.[47] Indeed, my daughter-in-law, Professor Janet Lyon, who has taught in a women's studies program at the University of Illinois in Urbana/Champaign, declared that the cultivation of a broad feminist sensibility was one of her prime goals in teaching.[48]

NWSA proclaimed this as its "fundamentally revolutionary position":

Women's studies owes its existence to the movement for the liberation of women; the women's liberation movement exists because women are oppressed. Women's studies, diverse as its components are, has at its best shared a vision of a world free not only from sexism but also from racism, class bias, ageism, heterosexual bias—from all the ideologies and institutions that have consciously or unconsciously oppressed and exploited some for the advantage of others.[49]

Opposition to women's studies and its description as "warrior feminism" was sharp within the university. "Was women's studies a discipline like history or English, requiring its own department?" feminists asked themselves.[50] Did it have the intellectual and theoretical matrix necessary for an academic discipline? Like urban studies and black studies before it, women's studies was challenged to prove that there was a substantial core of research and material to warrant college courses. In its early years, women's studies "was more Eurocentric but currently is now reporting to the new scholarship on third world women."[51] The implication from critics was that women's studies was basically feel-good therapy. Yet there existed a strong body of women's work, supplemented quickly by an astronomic productivity in the field.

Some feminist studies advocates denote that teaching is of more importance than male professors who concentrate on research. A 1991 NWSA "report to the profession," *Liberal Learning and the Women's Studies Major*, argued that "research is 'men's work'" whereas "teaching becomes like raising children."[52] Women's studies, the authors of the report argued "seeks to validate the worth of women's lives" and "nowhere is that clearer than in the feminist classroom."[53] Borrowing on research that indicates women learn better by studying cooperatively (*Women's Ways of Knowing*, 1990), it is noted that in feminist classrooms "there is much more attention to group work."[54]

The report proceeds to fourteen recommendations to strengthen women's studies in the university. Some of these indicate the fragile status these programs have on college campuses. The first recommendation is to "free women's studies programs from institutional constraints."[55] The lack of departmental status is a weakness of many of these programs. It should be recalled that the famed bandoliered black student protesters at Cornell in 1968 did not advocate revolution. They simply demanded a department for their black studies program. Departmental recognition is not a mere status symbol. It usually means protection from elimination and the allocation of more resources. And more resources was the second recommendation of the women studies report. Other issues included recruitment of faculty of color and more emphasis in curriculum of race and ethnicity.

CULTURAL STUDIES

A new amorphous discipline has emerged in academia: cultural studies. Cultural studies encompasses interrelated studies of culture, race, gender, and class. It is the hottest developing field on college campuses. There are standard reference works, such as the Simon During collection *The Cultural Studies Reader* and the Larry Grossbert/Cary Nelson/Paula Treichler volume *Cultural Studies*. There exist a major cultural studies journal in the United States, *Cultural Studies*, and two such journals in the United Kingdom. Publishers such as Routledge, New York University, and Greenwood devote series to cultural studies. Chain bookstores such as Barnes and Noble and Borders have large sections devoted to cultural studies.

Nevertheless, there are no cultural studies departments yet in the United States, nor any specific programs. There are cultural studies courses such as the History of Consciousness program at Santa Cruz University in California and the American Studies and Media Studies programs at New York University.

In *The Cultural Studies Reader* (1999, second edition), Simon During describes cultural studies as an "increasingly popular field of study."[56] He defines cultural studies as "the study of culture, or, more particularly, the study of contemporary culture."[57] During argues that there are "forms of analysis developed by the discipline."[58] He traces cultural studies to England in the 1950s and charts the various permutations of the discipline as it crossed the Atlantic.

The cultural studies field defies precise definition. One critic called cultural studies a "messy amalgam of sociology, social history, and literature, rewritten as it was a language of contemporary culture."[59] Michael Bérubé, who is an editor of a series called *Cultural Front* for New York University Press, admits that "cultural studies is not a unified movement . . . and not an academic discipline."[60] On the contrary, he argues, cultural studies "raids and unsettles the compartmentalized disciplines of traditional academic study."[61]

In his *Reader*, During gives a sample of the theories and concerns of cultural studies. His authors traverse many genres, from the neo-Marxist orientation of Theodor Adorno to the queer theory of Eve Kosofsky Sedgwick. Along the way we hear from Cornel West and "the new cultural politics of difference," Michel Foucault on the theory of power, Homi K. Bhabba on "the postcolonial and the postmodern," and bell hooks "on the promise of multicultural change."[62] At first glance, the book appears as a hodgepodge stew, but on closer reading one discerns a unity in these essays on the New World culture. To borrow an analogy from physics, cultural studies is an attempt across the disciplines for a unified field theory of culture.

The cultural studies movement is a strong, programmatic attempt of universities to address, in a unified fashion, the problems of a global universe. With the shrinking of continents through cheap air travel, CNN news, and the Internet, the global village becomes more of a reality day by day.

DISTANCE LEARNING

Perhaps the most disturbing trend in higher education is for universities—including urban universities—to develop high-tech televised instruction: distance learning. In an era of budget retrenchment, distance learning appears to be cost-effective, reaching more students for less. With the melding of computers and the Internet into such televised instruction in the last decade, there has been a rush toward the "new solution" to the problem of recruitment of students.

My university has been in the forefront of the distance learning movement, having fine-tuned a program in 1994 which reaches across Virginia and to sites in Washington, Arizona, North Carolina, Indiana, and the Bahamas. We now offer eighteen baccalaureate degree programs and nine master's degree programs via distance learning. Our distance learning program, TELETECHNET, is regularly hailed by state legislators and newspaper editorial writers.

Advocates of distance learning cite the ability to reach rural populations who otherwise could not attend a university. They point out that the technology is much advanced since the early televised instruction of the 1960s. Students have two-way communication with the instructor. Advocates point to the success of the British Open University as a model which has had over one hundred thousand graduates.[63] The only "pure" replication of the British Open University is the University of Phoenix, which is all distance learning without a mix of traditional classes.

Some advocates claim that distance learning is more effective in educating certain students. The president of my university, James V. Koch, wrote an op-ed piece for *The Chronicle of Higher Education,* citing research at our institution that "both male and female distance learning students earned higher grades than students in conventional versions of the same course."[64] He claimed that the difference might be due to the distance learning students being older, "more mature and more experienced than those who have just graduated from high school."[65]

The president of Teachers College at Columbia University, Arthur Levine, promoted distance and outline learning in the op-ed pages of the *New York Times.* Comparing education to a business, and citing the University of Phoenix which "is traded on the stock exchange," Levine warns that "Colleges and universities are not in the campus business, but the education business."[66] He urges colleges and universities to quickly get aboard the bandwagon for distance learning. Otherwise, "technological change has put higher education in danger of falling behind again."[67]

The critics of distance learning cite the elimination of "close faculty-student contact." That a good education can result from televised instruction, according to Michael Bérubé, constitutes a "naïve mindset."[68] Mass televised education, Bérubé argued in *The Chronicle of Higher Education,* "fails to address student writing and faculty advising." For Bérubé, "there's no way you can read and grade their papers, counsel them on their courses, work with them on their prospective careers, or write them letters of recommendations for jobs and postgraduate programs."[69]

But that is true of all large lecture classes in the hundreds, whether the traditional or the distance learning variety. My experience, having taught one televised class and a "virtual classroom" class, is that the most significant difference between a traditional class and a televised class may be a sense of anonymity on the part of the students and the professor in the televised class.

Some studies indicate that distance learning is not the "panacea" to higher education. Commissioned by the Alfred P. Sloan Foundation, six university distance learning programs were evaluated to determine their cost-effectiveness: Drexel University, Pace University, Pennsylvania State University, Rochester Institute of Technology, University of Illinois in Urbana/Champaign; and the University of Maryland. The bottom line was that these universities were not losing money on distance learning, but they were not reaping large rewards, either. They were close to the break-even mark. At Pace, traditional programs generated more revenue per student than the distance learning programs—a sizable $342 per student. Commenting on the Sloan studies, Bruce N. Chaloux, director of the Southern Regional Education Board's Electronic Campus, indicated that distance learning was not a "panacea, the silver bullet for responding to increasing demands for higher education."[70]

According to a survey of public attitudes toward higher education conducted in 2000 by the American Council of Education, "the public knows very little about distance learning."[71] Moreover, most "respondents were skeptical about the quality of such classes and degree programs."[72] And 83 percent preferred "the traditional, 'in-person' model of college education."[73] However, the public believes that distance learning courses "were cheaper than those offered on campus in the traditional way."[74]

In the age of the Internet and interactive television, technology has become the distinguishing feature of the new revolution in academia. Faculty members are urged to become computer-literate. Increasing numbers of middle-class students are growing up with computers in their homes-widening the educational gap with poor students who can't afford computers but must rely on those in public schools. Business depends heavily on the computer, perhaps echoing the insight of the media scholar Marshall McLuhan that "the medium is the message." Distance learning is part and parcel of this technological revolution, but it has severe limitations and is far from being a "panacea." Distance learning cannot replace the small seminar setting—the Mark Hopkins ideal of President James Garfield, two men sitting on a log, one being the redoubatble Hopkins, master teacher—and it is an unfortunate result of mass higher education with too few financial resources.

TOWARDS A SOCIALLY CONSCIOUS UNIVERSITY

What women's studies and cultural studies underline is the crucial assumption that knowledge—truth—is power. And they admit of a corollary assumption that knowledge is far from value-free. Women's studies programs liberate women, and cultural studies programs awaken one to the intersticed paradigm of a dominant culture in need of repair. Both programs have this as a function: to subvert the dominant paradigm. The purpose of this new university, therefore, becomes the inculcation in students of critical analysis and values to redress the inequities of the dominant contemporary society. Students, it is hoped, will become change agents. Is this purpose a violation of the idea of the university? Is not the aim of higher education to develop critical thinking and an understanding of the various components of culture? Is the university not an ivory tower separate from the world below?

Advocates of these programs think not. They would argue that the university is more than a temple of knowledge, that it has many rooms in it, and that preparing students to become change agents is part and parcel of knowledge itself. In the early 1970s my mentor and colleague Marilyn Gittell, who was then at Queens College, City University of New York, devised an innovative program in her newly created urban studies department to accept only students with a propensity to be change agents in the master's degree program. Some had not completed their baccalaureate work and were admitted on the basis of their community involvement. Similarly, my doctoral program at Union Graduate School, an accredited alternative degree program, had social action as part of its reason for being. The doctoral program in which I teach at Old Dominion University in urban studies/urban education has as its rationale that the university "has a major responsibility to contribute to the improvement and the quality of urban life and urban services in the Commonwealth by helping prepare people for leadership roles in a variety of public service professions."[75]

There are other examples of an edupolitics. The Brazilian educator Paulo Freire, in his influential book *The Pedagogy of the Oppressed* (1770), called for a school literacy program for poor peasants in Brazil to learn, through reading, of the oppression of their society, and to translate that knowledge into revolutionary action. This paradigm echoes John Dewey's call for reconstructing society as an aim of progressive education.

Correspondingly, the forerunners to women's and cultural studies— urban studies and black studies—staked out territory in redefining the identity of African Americans and addressing the programs of the city. Urban studies trains the new change agents that service urban America. Black studies programs give African Americans a usable past with which to master the present and the future. Urban university centers addressing the problems of the city have diminished in popularity. However, as of yet, women's studies centers have more of an educational than social action program. The university students in women's studies and cultural studies courses lack a link to direct action.

In *The Urban University in America*, I envisioned hope for the future of the socially conscious university. I wrote that, "in sum, the urban college and university has great potential in playing an increasingly important role in the life of the city."[76] To a large extent, depending on the university, that potential has been realized. Moreover, the university has *Adapted* to the shifts in the intellectual currents with women's and cultural studies and stayed the course with urban and black studies.

However, the American university is now confronted with the seductive power of distance learning. How that plays out will determine to a great extent if these advances are not wiped out by the televised classroom and the computerized online university.

NOTES

1. Maurice R. Berube, *The Urban University in America* (Westport, Connecticut: Greenwood Press, 1978), p. 14.

2. Brochure. Northeastern University, Boston, Massachusetts, 2000, p. 1.

3. Harold Enarson, Review of *The Urban University in America, Journal of Higher Education*, 1980, pp. 104–5.

4. Matthew Miller, "$140,000—And A Bargain," *New York Times* Sunday Magazine, June 13, 1999, p. 48.

5. Ibid.

6. Chester E. Finn, Jr., "What Ails Education Research," *Educational Researcher*, January/February, 1988, p. 5.

7. John Dewey, *How We Think* (Boston: D.C. Heath & Co. 1933), p. 11.

8. Henry Rosovsky, *The University: An Owner's Manual* (New York: W.W. Norton, 1991), pp. 105–6.

9. Ibid., pp. 85–86.

10. Rita Bornstein, "Back in the Spotlight: The College President as Public Intellectual," *Educational Record*, Fall, 1995, p. 5.

11. Ibid., p. 58.

12. Ibid.

13. Ibid.

14. Ibid., p. 62.

15. Berube, *The Urban University in America*, p. 60.

16. Ibid.

17. Ibid.

18. Stephen James Nelson, *Leaders in the Crucible: The Moral Voice of College Presidents* (Westport, Connecticut: Greenwood Press, 2000), p. 3.

19. Stanley O. Ikenberry and Terry U. Hartle, *Taking Stock* (Washington, D.C.: American Council on Education, 2000), p. 18.

20. Ibid.

21. Christopher J. Lucas, *American Higher Education: A History* (New York: St. Martin's Griffin, 1994), p. 237.

22. Ibid., p. 238.

23. Rosovsky, *The University*, p. 26.

24. Theodore Hesburgh, "Where are College Presidents' Voices on Important Public Issues," *Chronicle of Higher Education*, February 2, 2001, p. B20.

25. Nelson, *Leaders in the Crucible*, p. 188.

26. George Rupp, "Commencement Address," Columbia University, June 5, 2000, p. 3.

27. Ibid., p. 2.

28. Neil Rudenstine, "Commencement Address," Harvard University, June 8, 2000, p. 2.

29. Berube, *The Urban University in America*, p. 46.

30. Ibid., p. 48.

31. Ibid., p. 62.

32. *New York Times*, April 14, 1997, p. A1.

33. Old Dominion University, *The Village of the 21st Century* (Norfolk, Virginia: Old Dominion University, 2000), p. 1.

34. William Julius Wilson, *The Truly Disadvantaged* (Chicago: University of Chicago Press, 1987), p. 15.

35. Berube, *The Urban University in America* pp. 72, 75.

Beyond Modernism and Postmodernism

36. Urban Affairs Association, "Institutional Members," University of Delaware, January 24, 2001.

37. Berube, *The Urban University in America*, p. 83.

38. Manning Marable, ed., *Dispatches from the Ebony Tower* (New York: Columbia University Press, 2000), p. 23.

39. Ibid.

40. Ibid., p. 255.

41. Catherine R. Stimpson with Nina Kressnor Cobb, *Women's Studies in the United States* (New York: Ford Foundation, 1986), p. 10.

42. Ibid., pp. 42.

43. Ibid., pp. 16–17.

44. National Women's Studies Association, *Liberal Learning and the Women's Studies Major* (College Park, Maryland: University of Maryland, 1991), p. 17.

45. Beverly Guy Sheftal, *Women's Studies: A Retrospective* (New York: Ford Foundation, June, 1995), pp. 5, 11.

46. *1998–99 National Women's Studies Association Survey Report* (Champaign, Illinois: University of Illinois May 2000).

47. *Liberal Learning and the Women's Studies Major*, p. 14.

48. Interview with Janet Lyon, University of Illinois in Urbana/Champaign March 2, 2001 (telephone).

49. Stimpson, *Women's Studies in the United States*, p. 27.

50. Ibid., p. 29.

51. Sheftal, *Women's Studies: A Retrospective*, p. 21.

52. *Liberal Learning and the Women's Studies Major*, p. 13.

53. Ibid.

54. Ibid., p. 14.

55. Ibid., p. 17.

56. Simon During, ed., *The Cultural Studies Reader* second edition (London: Routledge, 1999), p. 1.

57. Ibid.

58. Ibid.

59. Michael Bérubé, *Public Access: Literary Theory and American Cultural Politics* (New York: Verso, 1994), p. 138.

60. Ibid.

61. Ibid.

62. During, *The Cultural Studies Reader*, pp. vi, v.

63. M.G. Moore and G. Kearsley, *Distance Education: A Systems View* (Belmont, California: Wadsworth Publishing Co., 1996), p. 42.

64. James V. Koch, "How Women Actually Perform in Distance Education," *Chronicle of Higher Education*, September 11, 1998, p. A60.

65. Ibid.

66. Arthur Levine, "The Soul of a New University," *New York Times*, March 13, 2000, p. A21.

67. Ibid.

68. Michael Bérubé, "Why Inefficiency Is Good for Universities," *Chronicle of Higher Education*, March 27, 1998, p. B5.

69. Ibid.

70. Sarah Carr, "Is Anyone Making Money on Distance Education?" *Chronicle of Higher Education*, February 16, 2001, p. A41.

71. Ikenberry and Hartle, *Taking Stock*, p. 19.

72. Ibid.

73. Ibid.

74. Ibid., p. 19.

75. Old Dominion University, "Doctor of Philosophy in Urban Services-Proposal to State Council of Higher Education in Virginia," Norfolk, Virginia, 1979, p. 3.

76. Berube, *The Urban University in America*, p. 16.

PART II

SCHOOLING

3

The Education of Diane Ravitch

Diane Ravitch became the first crossover educational historian in the last quarter of the twentieth century. Through her popular—but scholarly—histories and her appearances on the television media, Ravitch was thrust into a role of public personality. One observer remarked that "among the hundreds of educators, scholars and politicians . . . few have the stature that Diane Ravitch now has."[1] He noted that "Ravitch's name must be somewhere near the top of the Rolodex of every serious education journalist in the country."[2] Indeed, her main books have garnered largely favorable reviews in the major public reviewing forums read by literate America, such as the *New York Times* Sunday Book Review.

Ravitch has been described as "first and foremost an education historian, a teacher and a policy analyst."[3] She is the author of six books and co-editor of ten books and hundreds of articles. Her stance has been perceived as that of a "moderate-conservative on the spectrum of school politics."[4] Her educational histories rode a born-again conservatism in America that solidly rejected the basic principles and policies of John Kennedy's *New Frontier* and Lyndon Johnson's *Great Society* of the 1960s. Through her scholarship Ravitch gave a historical perspective to a conservative approach to school reform.

Ravitch's message was clear: American public schools were not fulfilling their potential and the school reforms that failure engendered were, for the most part, misguided. Ravitch became a prime theorist and advocate for clear national standards, a core curriculum as a base for cultural literacy that drew heavily on the contributions of European civilization, and a return to such traditional values as a fervent patriotism. Although she was an activist as well as a scholar—even venturing into a prominent role as a presidential aide in education—she, ironically, eschewed the political nature of education. Ravitch would write of her campaign for national standards that she "had become deeply concerned about the problems of their implementation and the possibility of their politicization."[5]

LIFE

Diane Ravitch was born in Houston, Texas, in 1939, the third of eight children, to parents who owned liquor stores and "were solidly middle class."[6] Her parents were Jewish, the mother an immigrant and the father the son of immigrants. Ravitch considered herself "a child of immigrants."[7]

She attended Houston public schools and performed well academically. In the Houston public schools she had "some wonderful teachers" and "some terrible teachers."[8] She loved to tell the story about her favorite teacher, Mrs. Ruby Ratliff, who taught her high school English. When Ravitch published her first book in 1975, she telephoned Mrs. Ratliff to "let her know she'd been my best teacher" because "she had given me so much wonderful poetry" and instilled a love of literature.[9] As Ravitch recounts it, Mrs. Ratliff "started crying" because she "really was a social studies teacher who was teaching out of license."[10] However, Ravitch also had bad memories of some teachers. "I vividly remembered the grade school teacher who shook me vigorously by the shoulders whenever I was late for school," she recalled, "and the one who tried (and failed) to make me into a right hander."[11]

Ravitch was sufficiently precocious to be admitted to an elite women's college, Wellesley in Massachusetts, where she studied political science. She considered the subject a "major waste of time."[12] In retrospect, she preferred history and literature as better preparation for the role of historian. At Wellesley she found the academic life "intellectual" and rigorous" and was "struggling for a B" whereas in public school she received As.[13] She realized that she "would never be best anymore" at Wellesley.[14] Nevertheless, Ravitch found Wellesley "a wonderful experience" which made her a "supporter of women's education."[15]

After college and marriage, Ravitch lived in New York City where she started her writing career in the sixties at *The New Leader* magazine. She had not yet enrolled in graduate school and considered herself "very much a late bloomer."[16] *The New Leader* is a small leftist publication that was militantly anti-Stalinist. Its tilt toward an obsessive anticommunism attracted funding from the Central Intelligence Agency (I wrote book reviews for *The New Leader*, among other intellectual journals of opinion, during that time, but stopped upon hearing of its CIA funding). As an editorial assistant Ravitch met writers at the magazine such as Daniel Bell, Irving Kristol, and Nathan Glazer, radicals who later emerged as neoconservatives. She considered her *New Leader* days also a "wonderful experience," since she was "introduced, in effect, to the great ideological and political battles that were going on at that time."[17] She regarded herself as a political naïf immersed in a world of radical politics that delighted in arguments.[18] She recalled in my interview with her in December of 2000 that the Deweyean philosopher "Sidney Hook urged me to be more argumentative."[19] Ravitch also wrote for *The Urban Review*, a creation of a federally funded think tank that analyzed developments in urban education.

Her turning point in "trying to figure out what I wanted to do for my life work" occurred shortly after the death of her second child from leukemia.[20] In 1968, as she was "recuperating from the death of a child," she "got very interested in writing a book" about the New York City teachers strikes and the community control movement.[21] Ravitch initially approached Mike Levitas, son of the founder of *The New Leader* and editor of the *New York Times Magazine*, to propose an article on the teacher strikes and community control. At that point Ravitch had written but a few book reviews for *The New Leader* and short pieces for *The Urban Review*. Levitas's reply was curt and sexist. He suggested that he might consider a piece along the lines of "I Danced with My Dentist."[22]

Ravitch then decided to return to college. She enrolled in Teachers College, Columbia University. Teachers College was the seat of the progressive education movement. Some notable educational giants had taught there, such as John Dewey, George Counts, and William Heard Kilpatrick. At Teachers College she came under the influence of Lawrence Cremin, arguably the leading educational historian of the era and, according to Ravitch, "the greatest historian of American education."[23] Cremin was the sympathetic historian of progressive education. Ravitch's "children went to a progressive school" in New York.[24]

RELATIONSHIP TO LAWRENCE CREMIN

Diane Ravitch's greatest influence was the educational historian at Teachers College, Columbia University, Lawrence A. Cremin. Cremin was the leading historian of his era, highly regarded for his sympathetic history of progressive education, *The Transformation of the School: Progressivism in American Education 1876–1957* published in 1962. It garnered for him both the Bancroft Prize in History and the Pulitzer Prize. Cremin was of the old school of historians who wrote histories on a grand scale—large ideas covering large historical eras. Ravitch was to be Cremin's most successful protégée following the master's template. "The teacher who most influenced me," she wrote, "was Lawrence Cremin."[25]

In the late sixties Ravitch, working as a "part-time researcher for the Carnegie Corporation," had "finished a report on the decentralization controversy that had paralyzed the New York City Schools during the fall of 1968" and "the controversy fascinated" her so that she "decided that I wanted to write a book about the history of the city's schools."[26] She was advised to meet with Cremin, described to her as "the dean of historians of education."[27] Ravitch then became a student of Cremin's at Teachers College. He revised her work-in-progress which became *The Great School Wars* and "the first published work accepted as a dissertation at Teachers College."[28] She found him to be "the best teacher I ever had" who "cared deeply about what he was teaching" so that "his passion was contagious."[29]

Cremin became her mentor, and Ravitch later noted that she "didn't publish anything until he had read it."[30] She would note of his mentorship that:

I knew that I would always be able to turn to him for advice the way that people turn to psychics and priests. He long ago became a permanent inhabitant of my brain, a mental and moral gyroscope, warning me whenever I wasted time or lurched too far in one direction.[31]

Indeed, Cremin functioned as a surrogate father and Ravitch "never made a career change without seeking his advice, because he was the only person I knew who could tell me what was right for me from my perspective."[32] For his part, Cremin worried that his guidance of Ravitch's scholarship might be too great so that he would not " 'get his thumbprints' on my work."[33] Ravitch would recall that Cremin remarked that "I had to develop my own voice, and he wanted me to have my voice, not his."[34]

But in one instance he played a larger role in Ravitch's work. Stung by the rising crop of young revisionist historians who painted their histories in non-Cremin miniature case studies and challenged his consensus perspective, he asked Ravitch to respond to their criticism. The rejoinder became the highly polemical *The Revisionists Revised*. Cremin reviewed the manuscript "as it evolved" always stressing "the importance of maintaining a civil, measured, tone."[35]

Ravitch initially regarded Cremin's magnum opus, *The Transformation of the School*, an "indispensable book" which was "path breaking" and "broke the mold" by linking progressive education as "an extension of the progressive movement in society."[36] Cremin was to view education "not solely in terms of what happens in schools."[37] He perceived education to be integrally linked to other "configurations of education, the networks of family, community, church, and school."[38] Ravitch would later disagree with Cremin that progressive education was beneficial to American education.

In a Freudian act, Ravitch was to kill the surrogate intellectual father with her book *Left Back*. Cremin was a child of the progressives, not only educated at progressive public schools in New York. He taught at the Vatican of progressive education, Teachers College, and married the daughter of a leading progressive educator there. *The Transformation of the School* was the historical bible of the progressive education movement. Ravitch's *Left Back* accuses the progressives of all that was wrong with American education.

THE GREAT SCHOOL WARS

I first met Diane Ravitch in the late 1960s when she was writing her first book, *The Great School Wars: New York City, 1805–1973, A History of the Public Schools as Battlefield of Social Change*. She was interviewing my boss, colleague, and mentor Professor Marilyn Gittell, Director of the Institute for Community Studies at Queens College, City University of New York.

Ravitch's position on community control was directly opposite to Gittell's and mine. The Institute was funded by the Ford Foundation to provide assistance to three experimental school districts in community control. Ravitch accurately described Gittell in *The Great School Wars*, as a person who "became known as an ardent advocate of community control."[39] Gittell and I had written in our edited book *Confrontation at Ocean Hill-Brownsville* that "the struggle for community control seems the best way of improving the quality of life in America."[40]

One need not rehearse the confrontation once again. More than a dozen books, here and abroad, have retraced that episode in the educational, racial, and political life of our nation (for example, Berube's *American School Reform* and Sophie Body-Gendrot's *Ville et Violence*). Simply put, community control was the product of African Americans who wanted to share in the educational power from which they had been disenfranchised because of elected school boards in the districts with only parents who had children in the schools eligible to vote. These boards would have final power to hire and fire, establish curricula, and raise funds. Community control was the first fleshing out of the Black Power phase of the civil rights movement. The first civil rights leader to promote the concept of Black Power, Stokely Carmichael, would write in his book *Black Power* that "control of the ghetto schools must be taken out of the hands of the professionals . . . the concept of community control has rooted itself in the consciousness of black people."[41]

Ravitch had a different perspective. She was sympathetic to the teachers union, headed by Albert Shanker, and its opposition to community control. She would write in *The Great School Wars* that "the drive for community control was a direct assault on the idea of the common school."[42] And she would conclude after her history of New York City educational politics that "the common school idea . . . has survived because it is appropriate to a democratic, heterogeneous society."[43] The black parents who first raised the question of a black curriculum for their students with placards demanding "Black Children Need Black Culture" during the confrontation were in direct conflict with the one-culture-fits-all proposition that Ravitch so ardently defended for over a generation.

The Great School Wars is an evenhanded account of the three great educational conflicts in New York City history. It is an admirable case study from the opposite side. Indeed, both *The Great School Wars* and *Confrontation at Ocean Hill-Brownsville* were used as source material for the Power! section of Henry Hampton's prize-winning video documentary on the history of the civil rights movement, *Eyes on the Prize*.

Perhaps the best part of Ravitch's book is the suggestion in the conclusion that these three educational wars, especially the community control movement, in essence went beyond educational politics. They were, in truth, painted on a larger canvas—a "search for community." But although Ravitch analyzes the first two wars—the creation of a public school system rather than a Catholic parochial one, and later the effort to oust corrupt politics from the schools at the turn of the century—in terms of a social, political, and economic matrix, Ravitch failed to fully grasp the importance of community to the disenfranchised minority in the ghetto.

Community control meant that blacks wanted a usable past in their effort to transform public schools into private schools. The ghetto was the antithesis of the community, the effort to create *civitas* of the Greeks and Romans, the holy "city on a hill" of the Puritans. The school was to become an all-purpose institution open all the time for the promulgation of black culture and a sense of community. The brutalizing poverty in the ghetto had made the idea of community the dream of black America.

Let us glimpse the rise of Diane Ravitch as measured by those reviews in the *New York Times*. Her first book, *The Great School Wars: New York City, 1805–1973*, (1974) was occasioned by the controversial community control movement in the late 1960s that divided New York liberals and radicals. George Levine of Columbia University would praise Ravitch for "her strenuous carefulness" about a "ferociously angry subject" which was "only five years away from the divisive and violent New York City school strikes."[44] Levine would remark about *The Great School Wars* that "it is hard to resist such scrupulousness, such common good sense."[45] The book was chosen by the Education Writers Association as best book of the year.

RAVITCH AND THE REVISIONISTS

The emergence of a new school of educational history in the 1960s and 1970s constituted "the 'golden era' in education history," according to forty educational historians gathered in March of 2000 under the Spencer Foundation to consider new directions in educational history.[46] Although invited, Ravitch did not attend due to scheduling problems. The distinguished panel of forty educational historians reminisced about those young historians.

Loosely labeled as "radical" revisionists . . . [who] . . . looked to a new kind of social history that focused on ordinary citizens and the travails of historical outsiders. These historians wrote about the politics of education, broadly defined, asking questions about who gained and who lost, whose interests were represented, and who were marginalized during earlier periods of educational reform . . . [they] . . . changed the direction of historical scholarship.[47]

The panel concluded that these revisionists captured "the attention of social historians, educational and social science researchers, policymakers, school reformers, and, to a certain extent, the lay public."[48] Politically to the left, the revisionists asked "provocative questions about the relationship of democracy to education, the role of school in the reproduction of social class, the origins and consequences of the bureaucratic organization of public schooling, the role of school in immigrant communities, and, to some extent, the struggles of people of color over access to schooling."[49] It was these revisionist historians that Lawrence Cremin implored Diane Ravitch to rebut.

My relationship to the revisionist historians was that of a fellow traveler. The revisionist Colin Greer was a friend, and I was a member of his doctoral committee at Union Graduate School shortly after his classic *The Great School Legend* was published in 1972. That same year I gave a sympathetic review to Michael Katz's collection of essays *Class, Bureacracy and the Schools* in *Commonweal* magazine, concluding that "Katz's book is sure to stimulate much thought."[50] Both Katz and Ravitch were to respect my book *Confrontation at Ocean Hill-Brownsville* (1969). "Maurice Berube and Marilyn Gittell," Katz wrote, "have provided a clear (as much as that subject can be) and intelligent book of readings representing a wide variety of points of view."[51] Ravitch was to consider that *Confrontation at Ocean Hill-Brownsville* "includes some of the most important documents of the period."[52]

Some of my work has followed in the path pioneered by the revisionists. Indeed, one reviewer of my book *The Urban University in America* (1978), considered me a "revisionist." Harold Enarson, then President of Ohio University, in reviewing my book stated that:

Today's urban universities, it is argued in this book, are obsessed with merito-cratic values, imprisoned by traditionalist faculty with elite views indifferent to neighborhood concerns. They perpetuate class stratification and racism, embody an agrarian bias, and neglect the city that sustains them.[53]

Being included with the revisionists constituted heady praise indeed, but, although I agreed with most of their criticism of American public schooling, I disagreed with their charge that little social mobility oc-curred in public schools. I sought to prove my point in my book *Education and Poverty*. Another reviewer of *The Urban University*, Professor Harvey Neufeldt, was more on target:

Revisionist writers questioned the notion that schooling had ever been—or by itself could be—utilized as an effective instrument for the eradication of poverty. Maurice Berube takes issue with the revisionists. It is not that he disregards the importance of meaningful reform in the political and economic realms outside the schools. However, he is convinced that education, in this case the Urban University, can make a difference for the urban community.[54]

Moreover, Neufeldt noted that "Berube bases his history on a variety of sources—he quotes Michael Katz, Samuel Bowles and Herbert Gintis, Colin Greer but also Diane Ravitch."[55]

In *The Revisionists Revised: A Critique of the Radical Attack on Schools* (1972), Ravitch clarified her own educational philosophy. By critiquing the work of the revisionists, Ravitch was able to solidify her own posi-tions. She adheres to a "democratic-liberal tradition in American edu-cation" that has as one of its chief aims the creation of a common culture. She found that the revisionists did not share that tradition but "they argue that the overall direction of American history has *not* been toward a just society."[56] She identifies some as "serious scholars" and others as "shrill polemicists" who are influenced largely by economic determin-ism"with a political orientation (that) ranges from Marxist to anarchist."[57] She claims that revisionism "began in 1968 with the publication of Mi-chael B. Katz's *The Irony of Early School Reform: Educational Innovation in Mid-Nineteenth Century Massachusetts.*"[58] But she also focused in her cri-tique on a handful of revisionist work: Colin Greer's *The Great School Legend*; Joel Spring's *Education and the Rise of the Corporate State*; Samuel Bowles and Herbert Gintis' *Schooling in Capitalist America*; Clarence Karier's *Shaping the American Educational State*; and Walter Fineberg's *Reason and Rhetoric*.

Ravitch reduces the assumptions of the revisionists to six propositions:

1. The public school "was used by the rich and the middle class as an instrument to manipulate and control the poor and working class."[59]
2. In the nineteenth century the campaign of school reformers to enroll "greater numbers" were "primarily middle-class morality campaigns."[60]
3. Revisionists had concluded that a great aim in seeking a common culture through public education had the adverse effect "to stamp out cultural diversity."[61]
4. Revisionists considered that there was little "upward mobility" by the children of the poor through school.[62]
5. They argued that bureaucracy was "deliberately selected" as a modicum of school governance resulting in racism, sexism, and class stratification.[63]
6. The revisionists considered schooling to "serve the needs of capitalism" such as "instilling work habits in future workers."[64]

These characterizations of revisionist writing are fairly accurate, and one feels that the revisionists themselves would consider them so, perhaps if written in a softer tone. The problem with *The Revisionists Revised* is that, in trying to disprove these scholars, Ravitch's argument runs thin on most of the six assumptions of the revisionists. The data collected by the revisionists *does* show that the nineteenth century school reformers were interested in saving the souls of poor folk through the schools. Moreover, the schools had historically tried to stamp out cultural diversity. Ravitch is on firmer footing when disputing social mobility in the schools, although as Colin Greer discovered, most of the students who were poor had failed in public schools.

Michael Katz, the leading revisionist, took exception to Ravitch's attack on his fellow revisionists. He claimed that "Ravitch's book added nothing to the historiography of education but were pure polemic.[65] Moreover, he felt that Ravitch portrayed the group as "intellectually and politically unified" whereas in fact they share "sharp differences of method, interpretation, and politics."[66] Katz pointed out that there is a contrast between the historical approach of the Cremin-Ravitch school of history and that of the revisionists. The revisionists used "new methods and applying social theory" which characterized the major direction of American history at the time, concentrating on case studies and employing quantitative as well as qualitative methodologies. Ravitch's work was old school, "a traditional narrative" of large eras and themes.[67] Ravitch contends that one problem with the direction of historical scholarship is that the work has been too minute, rendering innumerable historical case studies unimportant.[68]

Most important, Katz charged that Ravitch subscribed to a "different version of the American past" than the supercritical revisionists.[69] He considered her research to make her "one of the most articulate exponents of what I call the apologist case for American education, past and present."[70] However, Katz noted that Ravitch changed direction in her later work. She turned from her "complacent view of America's past" in *The Revisionists Revised* to her critical view of American education in *The Troubled Crusade* where, ironically, she "adopted the viewpoint of her former enemies and wrote a book more glum, less hopeful, than any of them."[71]

In conclusion, *The Revisionists Revised* stands as as a tome that perceives weaknesses in the work of the revisionist historians, but read along with their work, Ravitch's book underscores some of their strengths.

In reviewing *The Revisionists Revised*, Joseph Featherstone largely disagrees with Ravitch's assessment of the current crop of leftist educational historians, especially "her implicit argument that the revisionist are asking the wrong questions of the American past."[72] He would damn with faint praise the book as a "lucid and hard hitting polemic against a number of polemical historians."[73] His quarrel with Ravitch is over the philosophical assumptions of American society. The revisionist historians perceived education in America as suffering from racism, sexism, and classism. Featherstone finds *The Revisionists Revised* "a systematic confusion . . . of the defense of the values of pluralism and democracy . . . with a defense of the reigning style of corporate capitalism, which is another matter."[74]

The Troubled Crusade: American Education, 1945–1980, published in 1983, is Ravitch's finest book. Written with insight and an inordinate amount of fairness towards proponents with conflicting ideas, *The Troubled Crusade* garnered Ravitch the most critical scholarly and public support of any of her books. It was a major achievement at redefining American educational history, well written, and in the mode of the broad strokes of her mentor Lawrence Cremin. I have taught the book in my doctoral classes for nearly twenty years.

The basis of *The Troubled Crusade* is laid out in her title and her "assumptions," which are neatly presented in her introduction. Ravitch finds her historical organizing principle to be the idea that "equal opportunity became the overriding goal of postwar educational reformers."[75] She finds that battle, with its racial overtones, to be troubled and misguided. As a corollary, the schools still resonate with the clarion call of the progressive reformers of earlier decades to change the social order. "Probably no other idea has seemed more typically American," she writes "than the belief that schooling could cure society's ills."[76] As a result, she argues that "sometimes schools have been expected to take on responsibilities for which they were entirely unsuited."[77]

I find her assumptions to be partially true. My research has unearthed another historical perspective besides Ravitch's. In my book *American Presidents and Education* (1991), I discovered that the major drive for educational reform has been economic: to fine-tune a competitive global economy. Ravitch herself alludes to this development, but for her it is a subtext. "Technological change created a need for an educated people," she writes, "and educated people stimulated technological change."[78] For me the crusade for racial educational opportunity is the subtext to the postwar years into the end of the twentieth century.

Ravitch is correct is assessing that for many educators (as was the case with John Dewey), education is a religious calling whereby one can "dare change the social order" for the better. Ravitch believes that schools should pursue their original and narrow purpose of reading, writing, and arithmetic and leave the politics of social reform to other sectors of the society. But as Dewey pointed out, and later leftist scholars such as Michael Apple, Stanley Aronowitz, and Henry Giroux fleshed out—schoolteachers and school administrators bring with them to the classroom a "hidden curriculum" that subversively influences their charges. That "hidden curriculum" consists of the values by which the questions and the stated curriculum are structured. And for the most part, these teachers reflect middle-class majoritarian views—views that tend to uphold the status quo—and neglect those groups for whom social change is a necessity and for whom the Deweys and Giroux argue that schools must change the social order. As a case in point, consider David and Myra Sadker's research that *both* men and women teachers unconsciously teach to the boys, thus reinforcing gender discrimination.

Consequently, schools, Ravitch writes, are asked to do more than their initial mandate of teaching and learning. School administrators try to address the social problems of a pathology of poverty with free school breakfasts, teenage pregnancy and drug programs, AIDS information, antiviolence programs. She is correct in that diagnosis. My problem with that interpretation is that, by default, the schools have become the court of last resort. Organized religions have abdicated many of their responsibilities in that area, and the worlds of business and the military are not equipped to deal with social pathology. The problems are left to enlightened government and the schools.

Ravitch's trouble with the crusade for equal opportunity can be summed up in one word: race. She cannot get a handle on the thrust of the civil rights movement's primary goal to first equalize opportunity *through* the public schools. Ravitch devotes two chapters to race—one specifically dealing with the *Brown v. Topeka Board of Education* 1954 U.S. Supreme Court decision to outlaw school desegregation. For the most part, her depiction of the weakness of the decision is on target. The *Brown* decision did fail to specify an implementation decree, which crippled later efforts to desegregate schools. One must concede that the basis for the argument to desegregate, "reliance on sociological and psychological evidence," was shaky.[79] The lead lawyer for the National Association of Colored People (NAACP), Thurgood Marshall, had made psychologists Kenneth and Mamie Clark's famous "doll study" the basis of his legal challenge to the Supreme Court's *Plessy v. Ferguson,* which promulgated "separate but equal" facilities for African Americans. The "doll study" argued that psychological harm caused by racism motivated young black girls to choose white dolls over black dolls. Chief Justice Earl Warren, fresh from his guilt over imprisoning the Japanese during World War II while governor of California, agreed with Marshall and the Clarks. A decision overturning *Plessy v. Ferguson* was the result.

In relating the decision, Ravitch appears sympathetic to the convoluted logic of legal scholar Herbert Weschler of Columbia University Law School. Summarizing Weschler's position, Ravitch comments that "if segregated education is unconstitutional because social scientists say that it causes psychological harm to children, what happens if new sociological evidence emerges in the future to support a different finding?"[80] By successfully introducing the "doll study," Thurgood Marshall changed the rules of the game of the Supreme Court. No longer was evidence merely to be based on legal precedent. A division developed in the aftermath as legal scholars disputed the role of the Supreme Court. Should the court be a socially active court, or one that rules on the basis of the narrow confines of legal precedence?

Moreover, researchers could suitably question the qualitative methodology of the "doll study." Perhaps a more confounding variable existed in the children's selection of the dolls. But the supreme irony is that the "doll study" was replicated a generation after the surge of the civil rights movement and the results were the same. In a 1987 study black children chose the white dolls, and the researchers made the same conclusion from their study as had the Clarks. The children's choice of white dolls reflected a lack of self-esteem, caused by societal racism.[81]

The key to Ravitch's thinking on race rests with her assumption that civil rights means struggling toward a utopian society where color no longer has bearing. Ravitch believes that the visionary goal of "color blindness" was "mandated by the passage of the Civil Rights Act of 1964" which was the fruit of the blood and sweat of the civil rights movement.[82] In that respect, she seriously misreads the aim of the civil rights movement. Rather than proposing "color-blindness," the movement leaders, for the most part, argued for a "color sensitivity" that would redress the harsh aspects of racism. Ravitch felt that "the pursuit of color-blindness came to be characterized not as a noble goal, but as racism in a new form"—indeed, reverse racism.[83]

Ravitch was seriously out of step with the long march towards civil rights. Beginning with 1960s height of the civil rights movement, diversity became the key of national social policy. A host of reforms were sponsored by the federal government and the courts that celebrated programs to enhance diversity: affirmative action, bilingual education, equal rights for women, programs for the handicapped, redressing inequitable funding—much of which Ravitch found misguided. For example, Ravitch considered affirmative action tantamount to affirmative discrimination. "After a decade of discussion," she wrote, "few were convinced that the way to overcome a past in which benefits and burdens depended on race, sex, and national origin was to make permanent a system in which benefits and burdens depended on race, sex, and national origin."[84]

Yet Ravitch carried within her analysis some contradictions. Although considering "reformers, radicals and romantics" to be misguided in their efforts, she would perceive a case for diversity. In describing the community control movement in education (of which I was a part), she gave a balanced account of the aims of the civil rights leaders and their supporters and rendered a fair assessment of the movement's role:

The community control movement failed politically because it was perceived as a vehicle for black nationalism and racial separatism, thus threatening the fundamental notion of public schooling . . . Nonetheless, the movement gained a wide hearing for its critique of conventional educational and social ideas. It rejected the assimilationist goals of the integration movement and asserted the value of ethnic awareness. It disparaged the melting pot ideal of the common school in favor of the school as a reflection of the concerns and interests of the local community . . . But in their struggle for group recognition and solidarity . . . they violated the code of intergroup comity that permits a pluralistic society to function. Yet ironically . . . the community control movement left as its legacy the conviction that blacks must not be seen as an inferior cast, to be pitied and dispersed, but as an ethnic group asserting its demands and interests like others in a pluralistic society.[85]

Ravitch captured the key assumptions of the "radical reformers" of the 1960s. She found that many reformers had created a climate whereby "every new idea had a constituency, whether it was racial balancing of schools, parent participation, black community control or anything else that promised to break the grip of traditional practice."[86] Moreover, these reformers found that "there was little in the school worth preserving," that "anything innovative was bound to be better than whatever it replaced," and that "the only change worth attempting must be of a fundamental, institutional, systemic kind."[87] Indeed, I have heard many times during the community control struggle my colleague, Marilyn Gittell, a major player in community control, argue for systemic change rather than piecemeal change. In *The Troubled Crusade*, Ravitch favored "piecemeal change" rather than systemic "comprehensive change." She would ask how "did piecemeal change" get such a bad reputation?"[88] The irony was that, before the decade was out, Ravitch would ask for systemic change through a program of national standards.

Ravitch concluded her history of the "troubled crusade" with the admonition to temper one's faith in education. "If it seems naively American," she wrote as her last line in the book, "to put so much stock in schools, colleges and universities, and the endless prospect of self-improvement and social improvement, it is an admirable, and perhaps even a noble, flaw."[89]

Ravitch fared better in the *Times* with *The Troubled Crusade*. Ronald Berman, a former chairman of the National Endowment for the Humanities, rendered less a judgmental review than a book report on the main themes and highlights of the book. The strongest endorsement of *The Troubled Crusade* is his conclusion that the book "will be an especially valuable aid because it tells us three important things" about school reform.[90]

RAVITCH AND NATIONAL STANDARDS

Perhaps no other person in America has championed the national standards movement as strenuously and effectively as Diane Ravitch. As a tireless advocate of national standards in her many articles, as the Assistant Secretary of Research in the Department of Education in the George Bush administration concentrating on standards, and as the author of the book *National Standards in American Education: A Citizen's Guide*, Ravitch has had a profound impact on American school reform.

The development of the idea of national standards has been a collaborative project, first implanted in the Ronald Reagan administration and proclaimed with his successor George Bush. The idea of national standards has been the mainframe of the second wave in school reform. (See accompanying article "The Politics of National Standards.")

My acquaintanceship with the topic was brief but personal. In 1994 I was asked to be the guest editor of an issue of the academic journal *The Clearing House*, with my choice of topic and contributors. I chose national standards and contributors from both sides of the question. A deputy in President Bill Clinton's U.S. Office of Education agreed to write the first essay laying out the case for national standards. When the journal was about to go to press, I had recently been discharged from the hospital for having been operated for a blood clot on the brain, the result of an automobile accident. The editor of *The Clearing House* called in a panic to inform me that the Education deputy had reneged at the last minute on publishing his piece. We were left with an issue that might not be published. I called Diane Ravitch, relating my plight and informing her of my recent illness, and she sympathetically agreed to my reprinting some parts of her book on national standards, thus saving the issue.

National Standards in American Education continues Ravitch's pattern of presenting a clear, cogent argument. She has a short list of the advantages of national standards. "Standards can improve achievement," she writes, "by clearly defining what is to be taught and what kind of performance is expected."[91] Secondarily she perceives that national standards "serve as an important signaling device to students, parents, teachers, employers, and colleges."[92] Finally, she argues that national standards would constitute "consumer protection by supplying accurate information to students and parents."[93]

Ravitch attaches caveats to her version of national standards. She believes that standards must be *National*, and not locally developed as has occurred in the 49 states that are establishing standards. "There is no reason," she writes, "to have different standards in different states."[94] Moreover, she does not consider national standards a magic bullet by which American education would be miraculously restructured. There needs to be more money for schools and a host of other improvements. She warns that

National standards and assessment will accomplish little by themselves. Unless they are accompanied by better teaching, a better school environment, better instructional materials (including new technology), and more highly motivated students, student achievement will not improve.[95]

Of course, for an effective policy, national standards must correlate with national testing and even a national curriculum, neither of which are in place. They are being contemplated as policy in the near future. "Can national standards be set without establishing a national curriculum?" Ravitch asks.[96] Moreover, she realistically points out that "as matters now stand, the nation will have national content standards but not national testing."[97] She acknowledges that there is a "sort of national curriculum established by the five big textbook companies who dumb down texts to a low common denominator giving students sanitized versions of American history."[98] The United States does not have a national curriculum at a time when there is serious discussion about an international curriculum.

As the debate on having national standards—albeit not national in scope, but state standards—has been won by the standards advocates, there is beginning to be a cry for a multinational curriculum. In 1999, the idea of having a multinational curriculum was proposed by three professors of education. Two were from the United States, Walter Parker and John Cogan, and one professor was from Japan, Akira Ninomiya. In an article published in the *American Educational Research Journal*, they argued that "the time has come for the next curriculum to be in some respects a shared world curriculum, developed at least in part by a multinational team."[99] These authors of the article proceeded to organize a twenty-six-member international research team representing nine nations in four geopolitical regions to study the issue—East Asia, Southeast Asia, Europe, and North America.

President Bush did not offer legislation for national standards, although he set the stage for standards. Following Bush's lead, President Bill Clinton enacted legislation for standards, encouraging states to adopt *voluntarily* content standards, with a federal agency, the National Education Standards and Improvement Council (NESIC), "responsible for certifying the standards."[100] Each state, except one, has developed its own brand of content standards without regard for the other states.

Consequently, Ravitch's fervor for national standards has been tempered as time progressed in their development. She writes that

I began this book as an advocate of a particular approach . . . as time went by, events changed . . . my point of view. I continued to support strongly the idea of standards but had become deeply concerned about the problems of their implementation and the possibility of their politicization.[101]

As a case in point, Ravitch's initial support for Virginia's Standards of Learning (SOL) was diminished upon learning that Virginia's clear standards (as measured by the American Federation of Teachers) were to be assessed by multiple-choice test questions. She felt that a combination of multiple-choice questions, essay questions, and problem-solving questions would be the ideal measure of assessment of content standards.[102]

Ravitch's promotion of national standards cuts against the grain of her advocacy for piecemeal change. In *The Troubled Crusade* Ravitch criticized the "romantic reformers" for what she called their belief that the only significant change in education would have to be "systemic." She would ask rhetorically how piecemeal change got such a bad reputation.[103] Yet national standards equals systemic change. In my interview with her, she equivocated on the apparent contradiction. She called national standards a "direction education is going in, incrementally."[104]

A key to Ravitch's historical perspective is her envisioning the struggle in America for a common culture. She advocates "one common culture weaving the strands of the many separate cultures"—e pluribus unum (the one among the many).[105] In that regard, she was instrumental in persuading E.D. Hirsch, Jr., to write his best-selling 1987 book calling for a common culture, *Cultural Literacy: What Every American Needs to Know.*

"The single greatest impetus to writing this book", Hirsch revealed, "came from Diane Ravitch, who said simply that I ought to write a book, that I ought to call it CULTURAL LITERACY and that I ought to get it out as soon as possible."[106]

Ravitch abhorred the Afrocentrists who first appeared on the scene with the community control movement. The Afrocentric curriculum, she noted, was part of the "ethnic revival of the 1960's" and had "its intellectual roots in the ideology of the . . . black nationalist movement."[107] She regarded the self-esteem goal of Afrocentric curricula to be misguided, arguing "that it will detract from the real needs of the schools" such as well-paid teachers, small classes, summer programs, and the like.[108]

Ravitch's main Afrocentric opponent was Molefi Kete Assante, author of the 1990 book *Afrocentricity*. Assante argued that "Afrocentricity is the centerpiece of human regeneration" and "is the belief of the centrality of Africans in post modern history."[109] Consequently, for Assante "there is not a common American culture."[110] He believes that "the debate over the curriculum is really over a vision of the future of the United States."[111] Moreover, he sees in Ravitch's "common culture an additional myth to maintain Eurocentric hegemony."[112] He contends that "when Professor Ravitch speaks of mainstream, she does not have Spike Lee, Aretha Franklin, or John Coltrane in mind."[113]

Countering, Ravitch accuses *Afrocentricity* as being an "anti-intellectual book that is anti-white and homophobic."[114] She argues that Assante seeks erroneously "to promote a reverse racial supremacy debate over culture."[115] She feels that "a healthy debate was lost in the culture wars with *Afrocentricity*."[116] "Assante sees all white people alike," she maintains, "as oppressors and he ignores the severe critiques of the Eurocentric tradition made by such intellectual giants as Marx, Freud, and Dewey."[117]

LEFT BACK

Left Back: A Century of Failed School Reforms (2000) has been called Ravitch's "summa theologica."[118] Unfortunately, *Left Back* lacks the balance and persuasiveness of her other histories. *Left Back*, essentially, is Diane Ravitch's quarrel with John Dewey and the progressives. It is ironic that Ravitch, who was nurtured at Teachers College, Columbia—the main outpost for progressive education—and mentored by a sympathizer with the movement, Lawrence Cremin, would dedicate a huge tome to debunking the progressive legacy.

Ravitch locates everything that she thinks wrong with American education in the twentieth century on the doorstep of progressive education. She sees the legacy of progressive education and its disciples not as dead, as she had thought in *The Troubled Crusade*, but still alive and exerting a pernicious influence. She ends up ambivalent at best about Dewey but condemnatory of his disciples. However, she is kinder towards some neo-progressives such as Howard Gardner, Theodore Sizer, and Deborah Meier, since they are sympathetic to some aspects of the standards movement.

On the one hand, Ravitch finds in Dewey's progressive educational philosophy some positive aspects. She told Brian Lamb of C-SPAN television that Dewey is "very sensitive to children" and "makes people aware that how children learn is very important, that their motivation is very important and that their interest level is also very important."[119] Yet on the downside, she believes that Dewey "fuzzed things up an awful lot" so that "unsuccessful education movements came about because of people either misreading Dewey or sometimes reading him accurately but picking out the parts" they liked.[120]

In *Left Back* she also misreads Dewey. She argues that Dewey's prime interest in the public school is as the main change agent for social reform. Dewey's primary purpose, she writes, "was to make the schools an instrument of social reform."[121] True, Dewey had as one aim of his progressive educational philosophy to inculcate in students a social sense of improving society. But as one of his books indicates *How We Think*, Dewey first concentrated on thinking and learning, then its correlatives moral development, social development (as in reconstructing society), and aesthetic development. That was the essence of his philosophy and progressive education at its best.

Progressive education never got such a bad rap as Ravitch gives it in *Left Back*. Instead, she proposes her own list of neglected heroes, critics of progressive education, whose reputations she tries to resurrect, rather unsuccessfully, from the dustbins of history. But along the way, Ravitch offers excellent capsules of the contribution of these minor reformers and their ideological movements.

Does progressive education deserve the treatment Ravitch gives it? In my opinion—no. True, as Ravitch points out, the progressives were not able to educate the poor, since progressive education was more suited to—and more successful—in elite private schools. And she raises a serious question whether a common core curriculum dispatched by the progressives for a differentiated curriculum would not have been better in the long run. Surely, by differentiating into college courses, vocational courses, and general courses, poor and minority students could be—and were—tracked.

By concentrating on the weaknesses of progressive education, Ravitch neglects its strengths. No one can doubt that Dewey's definition of thinking and learning (solving *real* problems) constitutes a major contribution worldwide in education. The progressives—and neo-progressives—

stress high-level abstract thinking over rote memorization. The standards movement reintroduces rote memorization once again, and it is retrograde in that respect. Contrary to Ravitch, what is best about American education comes from the progressives. *Left Back* does not add to the author's reputation as a major educational historian.

In the *New York Times*, Sara Mosele read *Left Back* as a polemic against the progressives in education which was largely "persuasive."[122] But *Left Back* appeared to the reviewer as overkill, whereby Ravitch displayed a "sheer animus against the progressive tradition" which "may baffle lay readers."[123] Still, regarding school reform, Mosele concludes that "Ravitch's contribution in 'Left Back' is to help us realize how far we still have to go."[124] Ravitch's reviews were prominently featured in the *Times* Sunday Book Review. No other educational historian enjoyed such prominence in the *Times*.

RAVITCH AS ACTIVIST

The truth of the matter is that Ravitch's scholarly work falls into the realm of the politics of education. Joseph Featherstone's review of *The Revisionists Revised* was aptly called "The Politics of Education." Ronald Berman's review of *The Troubled Crusade* was titled "Scholastic Aims and Political Battles." George Levine's review of *The Great School Wars* was called "Education as a Reflex of Politics." Diane Ravitch views educational history from a contemporary political perspective.

Although Ravitch eschewed the turmoil of school politics, she found herself in the midst of controversies almost against her will. Her first foray in school politics occurred in 1989 with the battle in New York State over a social studies curriculum. As a strong proponent of high academic standards, and wary of injecting ethnicity in school curricula, she entered the political arena. The State Commissioner of Education had authorized a report on a new social studies curriculum. The report, *Curriculum of Inclusion*, charged that minorities had "been victims of an intellectual oppression" in the schools because of a "systematic bias toward European culture" in the curriculum that had a "terrible damaging effect" on minorities so that they "are not doing as well as expected" in public schools.[125]

Ravitch responded by condemning "an ethnocentric perspective that rejects or ignores the common culture."[126] She co-authored a manifesto with the historian Arthur Schlesinger ("Statement of the Committee of Scholars in Defense of History") which was signed by twenty-six other historians and published in New York newspapers. She later became involved in a similar state curriculum debate in California.

Ravitch followed those brief forays into school politics by reluctantly accepting a position in the U.S. Department of Education as assistant secretary for research in the Bush administration in 1991. She succeeded her friend, Chester Finn, Jr., who served in that post in the Reagan administration. "I was reluctant to enter government at all," she told a reporter from *The Chronicle of Higher Education*.[127] However, Lamar Alexander, new secretary of education, "made a very idealistic appeal." He said, "If you believe in making a difference, this is the time."[128] She would write of her experience in Washington that "we would start a crusade to improve education . . . and my assignment would be to put the topic of standards high on the nation's agenda.[129] She would recall that she "truly didn't want to do it; I liked working at my home in jeans."[130] Alexander's reply was that she could "start wearing a skirt" for the sake of making a difference in education.[131]

Ravitch served as assistant secretary for eighteen months until 1993. During that time her main emphasis was to develop national standards. The result was her book published in 1995, *National Standards in American Education: A Citizen's Guide*. She regarded her experience in Washington as mixed. Coming into "beltway politics" with "an outsider's perspective" she was seduced by the "glamour and political drama" of Washington and she "felt pride in doing public service."[132] But she was to be disappointed with the workings of the federal bureaucracy. She concluded that "the federal government will never be the leading edge of educational reform."[133] Most important, she felt that "she did more to promote national standards than anyone at the Department."[134]

Later, Ravitch was asked to join George W. Bush's campaign for the presidency against Vice President Al Gore in 2000. She was George W.'s education advisor until he refused to meet with the Log Cabin Republicans, a gay group of party members. In response to George W.'s action, Ravitch resigned from the campaign. "It was something I found to be intolerable," Ravitch told *Education Week*. "I believe in an inclusive approach to school politics."[135]

CONCLUSION

How does Ravitch's work stand up to the test of time? Most of her major books are out of print, such as *The Great School Wars, The Revisionists Revised*, and *The Troubled Crusade*. By contrast, many of John Dewey's books published before Ravitch was born, such as *Democracy and Education* (1916), are still being sold. Also, among her contemporaries Ravitch does not compare well. Howard Gardner's work, including his 1984 study *Frames of Mind: The Theory of Multiple Intelligences*, sells internationally, as does Carol Gilligan's 1983 study *In a Different Voice: Psychological Theory and Women's Development*. Granted that Gardner's and Gilligan's works were paradigm-shifting in transforming both psychology and education, but for a best-selling historian's work to disappear raises questions. Perhaps the reason for the fading of Ravitch's work is the anchoring of her histories in contemporary controversies and viewing history from the school politics of her day.

On the other hand, other major educational historians who have not based their work on a contemporary perspective are no longer in print. Lawrence Cremin's 1962 masterpiece, *The Transformation of the School*, and revisionist Michael B. Katz's 1969 microanalytic classic, *The Irony of Early School Reform*, are both unavailable to the book buyer. This makes one wonder why educational histories have lost their appeal to young scholars while classics in psychology, such as Gardner's and Gilligan's, endure, as do the works of philosopher John Dewey. A simpler and more cogent reason, one suggested by Ravitch herself, is that educational history is declining as a requisite course in American colleges and universities; thus, there exists little demand for the books.

The irony of ironies is that this quiet historian, who finds the shrill world of educational politics to be abhorrent, would become the first major educational historian to have enormous policy impact on educational reform. Her intellectual involvement and scholarship have made her the most vocal supporter of the national standards movements. She summed up her efforts by stating that "national standards is the direction that education reform will take in the future; its course will not be reversed and it will progress incrementally."[136] That effort alone will guarantee her a place in the history of American education. Diane Ravitch has demonstrated that the pen can not only record history, but create it.

But then again there are the books. Surely, *The Great School Wars* and *The Troubled Crusade* will be read by serious scholars of American educational history, whatever their political persuasions. Diane Ravitch will take her place in the pantheon of educational historians, along with her mentor, Lawrence Cremin, and her opposites, Michael Katz and his fellow revisionists. American educational history has never been so rich in perspectives and relevance. Theirs was truly a golden age.

NOTES

1. Peter Schrag, "The Education of Diane Ravitch," *The Nation*, October 2, 2000, p. 31.
   2. Ibid.
   3. Ibid.
   4. Ibid.
   5. Diane Ravitch, *National Standards in American Education: A Citizen's Guide* (Washington, D.C.: The Brookings Institute, 1995), p. xiii.
   6. Brian Lamb Interview with Diane Ravitch, *Booknotes*, C-SPAN Television, September 15, 2000, transcript, p. 7.

7. Ibid.

8. Ibid., p. 3.

9. Ibid., p. 6.

10. Ibid.

11. Diane Ravitch, "Lawrence A. Cremin," *The American Scholar*, Winter, 1992, p. 83.

12. *Booknotes*, p. 8.

13. Ibid., p. 9.

14. Ibid., p. 7.

15. Ibid.

16. Ibid.

17. Ibid., p. 8.

18. Maurice R. Berube Interview with Diane Ravitch, New York City, December 4, 2000.

19. Ibid.

20. Berube Interview with Diane Ravitch.

21. *Booknotes*, p. 8.

22. Ibid.

23. Berube Interview with Diane Ravitch.

24. *Booknotes*, p. 9.

25. Ibid., p. 11.

26. Diane Ravitch, "Lawrence A. Cremin," *American Scholar*, p. 83.

27. Ibid.

28. Ibid.

29. Ibid.

30. Ibid., p. 86.

31. Ibid., p. 87.

32. Ibid., p. 89.

33. Ibid., p. 97.

34. Ibid.

35. Ibid.

36. Ibid., p. 84.

37. Ibid.

38. Ibid., p. 85

39. Diane Ravitch, *The Great School Wars: New York City, 1805–1973, A History of the Public Schools as Battlefield of Social Change* (New York: Basic Books, 1975), p. 341.

40. Maurice R. Berube and Marilyn Gittell, eds., *Confrontation at Ocean Hill-Brownsville* (New York: Praeger, 1969), p. 10.

41. Stokely Carmichael and Charles V. Hamilton, *Black Power: The Politics of Liberation* (New York: Vintage Edition, 1992), p. 47.

42. Diane Ravitch, *The Great School Wars*, p. 397.

43. Ibid., p. 402

44. George Levine, "Education as a Reflex of Politics," *New York Times Sunday Book Review*, May 12, 1974, p. 4.

45. Ibid.

46. Ruben Donato and Marvin Lazerson, "New Directions in American Ed-

ucational History: Problems and Prospects," *Educational Researcher*, November, 2000, p. 5.

47. Ibid.

48. Ibid.

49. Ibid.

50. Maurice R. Berube, "The End of School Reform," *Commonweal*, April, 1972, p. 122.

51. Michael Katz, *Class, Bureaucracy and the Schools* (New York: Praeger, 1972), p. 152.

52. Diane Ravitch, *The Great School Wars*, p. 430.

53. Harold Enarson, Review of *The Urban University in America, Journal of Higher Education*, Jan./Feb., 1980, p. 79.

54. Harvey Neufeldt, Review of Maurice R. Berube, *The Urban University in America, Educational Studies*, Summer, 1979, pp. 206–7.

55. Ibid., p. 208

56. Diane Ravitch, *The Revisionists Revised* (New York: Basic Books, 1977), p. 32.

57. Ibid.

58. Ibid.

59. Ibid., p. 57.

60. Ibid.

61. Ibid.

62. Ibid.

63. Ibid.

64. Ibid.

65. Michael Katz, *Reconstructing American Education* (Cambridge, Massachusetts: Harvard University Press, 1987), p. 145.

66. Ibid., p. 146.

67. Ibid.

68. Berube Interview with Diane Ravitch.

69. Michael Katz, *Reconstructing American Education*, p. 146.

70. Ibid.

71. Ibid., pp. 150, 158.

72. Joseph Featherstone, "The Politics of Education," *New York Times Sunday Book Review*, June 18, 1978, p. 9.

73. Ibid.

74. Ibid., p. 40.

75. Diane Ravitch, *The Troubled Crusade: American Education, 1945–1980* (New York: Basic Books, 1983), p. xi.

76. Ibid., p. 79.

77. Ibid., p. xii.

78. Ibid., p. 10.

79. Ibid., p. 129.

80. Ibid.

81. *New York Times*, August 31, 1987, p. A9.

82. Diane Ravitch, *The Troubled Crusade*, p. 145.

83. Ibid., p. 114.

84. Ibid., p. 292.

85. Ibid., p. 174

86. Ibid., p. 237.

87. Ibid., pp. 237–38

88. Ibid., p. 261

89. Ibid., p. 330

90. Ronald Berman, "Scholastic Aims and Political Battles," *New York Times Sunday Book Review*, September 18, 1983, p. 35.

91. Diane Ravitch, *National Standards*, p. 25.

92. Ibid.

93. Ibid.

94. Ibid.

95. Ibid., p. 35.

96. Ibid., p. 30.

97. Ibid., p. 31.

98. Berube Interview with Diane Ravitch.

99. Walter C. Parker, Akira Ninomiya, and John Cogan, "Educating World Citizens: Toward Multinational Curriculum Development," *American Educational Research Journal*, Summer, 1999, p. 120.

100. Diane Ravitch, *National Standards*, p. 29.

101. Ibid., pp. xii–xiii.

102. Berube Interview with Diane Ravitch.

103. Diane Ravitch, *The Troubled Crusade*, p. 261.

104. Berube Interview with Diane Ravitch.

105. Diane Ravitch, "Multiculturalism: E Pluribus Unum," in Paul Berman, ed., *Debating P.C.* (New York, Laurel: 1992), p. 274.

106. E.D. Hirsch, Jr., *Cultural Literacy: What Every American Needs to Know* (New York: Vintage, 1988), p. viii.

107. Diane Ravitch, "Multiculturalism: E Pluribus Unum," p. 275.

108. Ibid., p. 289

109. Molefi Kete Assante, *Afrocentricity* (Trenton, New Jersey: African World Press, Inc., 1990), p. 1.

110. Molefi Kete Assante, "Multiculturalism: An Exchange," in *Debating P.C.*, p. 308.

111. Ibid.

112. Ibid., p. 305.

113. Ibid.

114. Berube Interview with Diane Ravitch.

115. Ibid.

116. Ibid.

117. Ibid.

118. Peter Schrag, "The Education of Diane Ravitch," *The Nation*, October 2, 2000, p. 31.

119. Brian Lamb Interview with Diane Ravitch, *Booknotes*, p. 1.

120. Ibid., p. 2.

121. Diane Ravitch, *Left Back: A Century of Failed School Reforms* (New York: Simon and Schuster, 2000), p. 57.

122. Sara Mosle, "The Fourth R," *New York Times Sunday Book Review*, August 27, 2000, p. 7.

123. Ibid.

124. Ibid.

125. New York State Task Force on Minorities, *A Curriculum of Inclusion* (Albany: New York Department of Education, July, 1989), p. iv.

126. Diane Ravitch, "Multiculturalism," p. 292.

127. *The Chronicle of Higher Education*, September 11, 1991, p. A51.

128. Diane Ravitch, "Adventures in Wonderland: A Scholar in Washington," *The American Scholar*, Autumn, 1995, p. 497.

129. Ibid.

130. Berube Interview with Diane Ravitch.

131. Ibid.

132. Diane Ravitch, "Adventures in Wonderland," p. 500.

133. Ibid.

134. Ibid.

135. *Education Week*, January 12, 2000, p. 23.

136. Berube Interview with Diane Ravitch.

4

The Politics of School Reform

An examination of the history of public school reform in America reveals that certain variables are uniformly consistent with each of the three great school reform movements. These major reform movements are the progressive education movement at the turn of the century, the equity reform movement of the 1960s and 1970s, and the excellence reform movement of the 1980s and 1990s. Each of these respective movements was shaped and defined by outside societal forces: progressive education by progressive social reform, equity reform by the civil rights movement, and excellence reform by foreign economic competition.

One can identify characteristics common to all three movements. Reformers in each movement sought comprehensive change in the public school system. Emphasis was on innovation, replacing the old with new and better experimental programs. Reformers based their ideas on the rising scholarship in America. These reformers constituted a new breed in academia, that of the scholar activist. Most important, the reformers of the first two movements were, for the most part, political liberals or radicals, whereas the excellence reformers were primarily political conservatives. Finally, with the emergence of the United States as the dominant technological society after World War II, American presidents became increasingly involved in establishing a national educational agenda despite constitutional constraints.

The clamor for comprehensive educational change has a long history.

John Dewey and his fellow progressive education reformers advocated no less than transforming the entire American educational system. Their aim was to replace the existing method of rote memorization with a liberating educational philosophy and practice that went beyond the intellectual and developed the full potential of students. The key phrase was the "whole child." By this Dewey and his fellow reformers meant the intellectual, moral, artistic, and social potential of students. They disapproved of a sole emphasis on developing intellectual ability without the development of character or the impulse to change society. (The social aim was later misinterpreted to mean life-adjustment; a dilution that signaled the end of progressive ideas by the 1940s.)

The whole child's potential was to be *developed* with an emphasis on learning by doing. Thinking and learning, Dewey proposed, only occurs when one is problem solving. Thus, the idea of "critical thinking" became the slogan of a characteristically American brand of education. Progressive education drew much from the philosophy of American pragmatism and its high priests, William James and John Dewey. It was also the result of the rising scientific scholarship in America. The new science of psychology, of which James was an early and major proponent, posited that the mind and learning were not fixed but could be developed. The progressive concept of development came under attack a century later with the excellence reformers. In retrograde fashion, excellence reformers repudiated progressivism to revert to content-specific curricula. E.D. Hirsch, Jr., would attack Dewey as being "deeply mistaken" about education.[1] Hirsch characterized Dewey as "the writer who has most deeply affected American education history and practice."[2]

It was no accident, therefore, that the progressive reformers were primarily political liberals and radicals. Their educational ideas were born in an era of strong social protest, with the larger political reform of progressivism. In the background, the socialism of the white ethnic immigrants in the cities was ever present. Moreover, John Dewey became the first major scholar in American educational history to be also an educational and political activist. Dewey embodied his educational ideas in laboratory schools. In addition, he was a major political actor, involved in the rise of teacher unionism and civil liberties. He even created his own political party, which occupied a position somewhere between liberals and the socialists on the political landscape.

Progressive education distinctly shaped American education. Nonetheless, it had limitations. Despite the high moral tone of many of the progressives, such as Dewey and George S. Counts, progressive education did not succeed in educating the immigrant poor. Part of the problem was that progressive schools were first developed in private, elite schools. Also, there was the difficulty in educating the poor. It was left to the equity reform movement, fueled by the civil rights movement, to more fully address the education of the poor. Consequently, progressive reform failed to address the issue of finance, which equity reformers addressed. Progressive education was, for the most part, cost-neutral.

THE EQUITY REFORM MOVEMENT (1954–1983)

The next major public school reform movement occurred mainly during the 1960s. The equity school reform movement was shaped by the civil rights movement and emphasized the education of the poor, thus attempting to complete the unfinished agenda of the progressive education reformers. Indeed, neoconservative educational historian Diane Ravitch would correctly perceive that the equity reformers of the sixties comprised a "new progressivism" that "grew out of the bitter reaction against the inadequacies of the American public schools educating minority children."[3]

The equity reformers had much in common with their progressive forebears. They were, for the most part, political liberals or radicals energized by the civil rights movement. They stressed innovation and comprehensive change. For the poor, the educational system was dysfunctional. In the cities, the poor translated into a minority poor with the mass migration in the 1950s of the white middle class to the suburbs. (Ironically, one of the goals of the civil rights and equity reform movements—affirmative action—would result in a rising black middle class that by the 1980s would follow the white middle class to the suburbs, thus further destabilizing urban ghettoes.)[4]

In her history of education after World War II, *The Troubled Crusade*, Ravitch further characterized the equity reform movement:

Every new idea had a constituency, whether it was racial balancing of schools, parent participation, black community control, or anything else that promised to break the grip of traditional practice . . . The underlying assumptions in the various approaches were, first, that there was little in the schools worth preserving; second, that anything innovative was bound to be better than whatever—it replaced; third, that the pathology of the schools was so grave that the only change worth attempting must be of a fundamental institutional, systematic kind; and fourth, that the way to change society . . . was to change (or abandon) the schools.[5]

Ravitch's assessment of the equity reformers was a fair one. My colleague and mentor, Marilyn Gittell, a major figure in the community control movement, often stated that only far-reaching systemic—that is, comprehensive change—in school governance was needed to reform the urban public schools. Indeed, a key element of President Richard Nixon's Experimental Schools Program of the early 1970s was a mandate to de-

velop model schools for "comprehensive change."[6] Ravitch, who considered the Nixon initiative "one of the most ambitious federal efforts to
reform schools," nonetheless would bristle at "comprehensive change"
and wonder "how, then, did piecemeal change get such a bad reputation."[7]

In another historical irony, Ravitch, who questioned comprehensive
change with the equity reformers, would advocate it as an excellence
reformer in the 1990s. Moreover, her criticism of scholars-turned-activists
was forgotten when she became the assistant secretary for research in
the U.S. Department of Education in the Bush administration, succeeding
another scholar-turned-activist, Chester Finn, Jr.

George Bush revived the Nixon Experimental Schools Program with
his *GOALS 2000* legislative proposal. The Bush initiative called for 535
New American Schools that would qualify for some $150–200 million for
innovative programs that would "break the mold" of public education.[8]
These experimental schools would be selected on the basis of innovative
programs that would hopefully chart a new course in American education, In short, the New American Schools, much like the Nixon experimental school program, would seek comprehensive change through
experimental programs that were innovative in nature.

The equity reform movement resulted in a plethora of new ideas em-
bodying systematic change. The key assumption of equity reformers was
enunciated by Harvard psychologist Jerome Bruner in his popular 1960
book *The Process of Education*. Bruner declared that "any subject can be
taught effectively in some intellectually honest form to any child at any
stage of development."[9] Bruner's optimism was soon tempered by the
release of test scores in major cities as a result of pressure by civil rights
groups. It was revealed that minority youths were failing in massive
numbers. Nonetheless, equity reformers sought to find a way to better
educate the poor. They also held a romantic concept of the poor. Like
the progressives, they perceived the poor as decent people brutalized by
poverty.

First, there were issues of governance. The civil rights movement declared education to be a chief priority in the famed 1954 *Brown v. Topeka
Board of Education* U.S. Supreme Court decision. Black activists initially
wanted school integration as a means to create opportunity for black
youths. Later, when school integration dimmed as a reality in the major
cities, they sought control of the schools—community control. Community control simply meant that in the urban ghettoes school boards
would be elected by black parents with children in the public schools.
These boards would have power over policy, such as personnel, curriculum, and budget. It was the first time that finance was mentioned as
instrumental to reform.

Other pedagogical strategies developed. Pedagogical approaches such as the British Open School, bilingual schools, Montessori, Summerhill, and free alternative schools were but some of the many educational ideas that were entertained. Educational books became popular, concerned with the need to educate an urban minority poor. Nat Hentoff's book of a New York City principal was titled *Our Children Are Dying*. Charles Silberman's best-seller *Crisis in the Classroom* was originally titled *Murder in the Classroom*. Jonathan Kozol's account of his teaching year in the Boston public schools, which won him the only National Book Award for a book on education was equally provocatively titled *Death at an Early Age: The Destruction of Hearts and Minds of Negro Children*. The emphasis was on death of the mind.

This educational reform movement was taken up by the White House. President Lyndon B. Johnson was sympathetic with educational reform for the poor. A former schoolteacher whose mother also was a former schoolteacher, Johnson believed that education was the chief way to enable a person to move out of poverty. In constructing the blueprint for his Great Society, Johnson concentrated on education as the main avenue out of poverty. He told his circle of aides:

This is going to be an education program. We are going to eliminate poverty with education, and I don't want anybody ever to mention income redistribution. This is going to be something where people are going to *learn* their way out of poverty. (Paraphrased).[10]

Consequently, Johnson helped enact sixty education bills into law, including the historic first federal aid to education act. The key was targeting the children of the poor. Head Start, a preschool program for the poor, accompanied the 1965 Elementary and Secondary Education Act as the linchpin of the Johnson administration. Johnson wanted to be thought of as an "education president," a term he coined for himself.[11] With some justification, Johnson stands alone in his efforts to address the educational needs of American society. The Great Society, he declared, would be forged "in our cities, in our countryside, and in our classrooms."[12] Indeed, his aides remember his obsession with education:

Nothing was in his thoughts more often. He sought guarantees that every boy or girl in the United States 'could have all the education he or she can take.' He was actually superstitious about the subject, and at times one expected him to advocate college as a cure for dandruff or university as a specific for sore throats.[13]

The equity reformers introduced money as a key ingredient to improve the education of the poor. Early intervention programs such as Head Start required enriched services, making them more costly. Consequently, the Johnson administration provided a historic high of 9 percent of the funding of education nationwide.

It was no accident, therefore, that the equity reform movement would give rise to finance reform. In the late 1960s in California, a distinct group of equity reformers challenged the system of funding public education. Since much of local and state funding of public schools was based on deriving revenue from property taxes, the result was an inequitable school system. Disparities of rich and poor were common in each state, and states spent differing amounts in education. For example, property-rich Fairfax County, Virginia, a suburb of Washington, D.C., raises more money for schools than the county of Accomack, Virginia, comprised of poor farmland. Similarly, New York outspends Mississippi in public education.

In 1971, the California Supreme Court in the *Serrano* decision declared the property tax to be discriminatory. The finance reformers received a setback from the U.S. Supreme Court in 1974 in the *Rodriguez* decision. In a 5–4 ruling, Justice Lewis Powell, writing for the majority, concluded that "education, of course, is not among the rights afforded explicit protection under our Federal constitution."[14] Undaunted, finance reformers continued their struggle for equity in public school funding through the state courts for the next twenty years. As of this writing, some twenty-six states had their school finance systems challenged in state courts.

In summary, the equity reform movement sought comprehensive change through innovative programs with the main emphasis on educating the poor. That objective was defined by the pressure of the civil rights movement. Moreover, in seeking to address the unfinished agenda of progressive educators in educating the poor, equity reformers considered the issue of school finance. The assumption of equity reformers was that programs to help educate poor people required more money. This assumption led to the realization that the entire system of public education was inherently unequal, since much of it was based on revenue from property taxes.

THE EXCELLENCE REFORM MOVEMENT (1983–1994)

Equity school reform dominated the national scene for nearly twenty years. Despite the accession of Republicans to the White House (counterbalanced by a Democratic Congress), national educational policies, which were voluntarily followed by the states, were directed at educating the poor. However, the civil rights movement had been checked in its influence for a variety of reasons. Much of the black leadership had either been killed or become burned out. In 1968 the nation elected a conservative president in Richard Nixon, signaling the ascendancy of a conservative constituency in America that was to culminate with the election of Ronald Reagan in 1980. With the demise of the civil rights movement, the equity school reformers lost their chief constituency in advocating their brand of school reform.

Most important, the nation was to be beset with the decline of the American economy, a problem that was to supercede civil rights in America's attention. For more than a generation succeeding World War II, America experienced prosperity and worldwide dominance. Now, the American economy was in fast decline. The causes were varied. First, economic competition from rebuilt economies such as those of Japan and West Germany challenged American technological preeminence. Second, American business had shifted economic philosophy from long-term gains to short-term profits. The amount of money invested in plant modernization declined. Third, American cold war policy was directed at the military sector at a time when foreign competitors could concentrate wholly on domestic products. Fully 50 percent of Americas scientists— the best and brightest—were in defense and space programs. Moreover, the American military presence throughout the world became increasingly expensive as the Reagan military buildup propelled a national budget deficit from $79 billion in Jimmy Carter's last year to an average $186 billion in Reagan's first four years.[15]

The American public became anxious over America's economic decline. For example, industrial growth in the United States for the years 1972–78 grew only by 1 percent, compared to Japan's industrial growth of 5 percent.[16] Consequently, the United States dropped from second to fifth at that time in per capita gross national product.

Who was at fault for America's economic decline? At first, the focus was on American business. A publishing cottage industry quickly emerged whereby American business was perceived as shortsighted compared to such foreign competitors as Japan. However, blaming the corporate culture soon gave way to blaming the schools. If one document can be acknowledged as starting the excellence reform movement, it was the U.S. Department of Education's provocative thirty-six-page "study" *A Nation at Risk: The Imperative for Educational Reform* released in the spring of 1993.

A Nation at Risk was essentially a political document. The idea for a presidential commission to "examine" public education was wholly that of Secretary of Education Terrell Bell. Bell commissioned the "study" and empanelled a group of educators to report on the state of American education. Bell took this action without the presidential sanction of Ronald Reagan and his aides. Indeed, Reagan had little interest in reforming public education. As governor of California in 1970, he endorsed vouchers for private and parochial schools. In 1982, he sought a constitutional amendment for school prayer which the Democratic Congress successfully rebuffed. Moreover, he favored tuition tax credits for parents with children in private and parochial schools. Most important, he wanted to eliminate all federal funding to education. Nevertheless, Bell agreed to become secretary of education in the hope that he could, "persuade . . . (Reagan) to endorse what must be done for the learning society that America must become if it is to survive and achieve its destiny."[17] Reagan became a convert as the polls indicated that educational reform was the second most important issue in the 1984 presidential election.[18]

A Nation at Risk had the clearest link to an outside societal force:

History is not kind to idlers. The time is long past when America's destiny was assured simply by an abundance of natural resources and inexhaustible human enthusiasm, and by our relative isolation from the malignant problems of older civilizations. The world is indeed one global village. We live among determined, well-educated, and strongly motivated competitors. We compete with them for international standing and market, not only with products but also with the ideas of our laboratories and neighborhood workshops. America's position in the world may once have been reasonably secure with only a few exceptionally well-trained men and women. It is no longer.

The risk is not only that the Japanese make automobiles more efficiently than Americans and have government subsidies for development and export. It is not just that the South Koreans recently built the world's most efficient steel mill, or that American machine tools, once the pride of the world, are being displaced by German products. It is also that these developments signify a redistribution of trained capability throughout the globe. Knowledge, learning, information, and skilled intelligence are the new raw materials of international commerce and are today spreading throughout the world as vigorously as miracle drugs, synthetic fertilizers, and blue jeans did earlier . . .

Learning is the indispensable investment required for success in the "information age" we are entering.[19]

The charges of *A Nation at Risk* were mainly fivefold. First, American students were last in a series of academic indices as compared to students in eighteen other industrialized nations. Second, American students recorded a precipitous drop in scores on the Scholastic Aptitude Tests, a necessary national voluntary examination for entry into colleges, between the years of 1960 and 1980. Third, seventeen-year-old students had poor inferential ability. Fourth, students were falling behind in science learning. Fifth, there was a rise in illiteracy. There was no mention of funding.

The statistics of this "excellence" study were challenged by a handful of scholars, mostly equity reformers. First, these scholars argued that international comparisons with the United States were skewed because the samples were incomparable. The U.S. educational system is open rather than selective. National tests such as those in the European and Japanese industrialized countries "screen out," whereas the United

States, without such tests, provides more mobility. When controlled for samples, U.S. students rank much higher. The drop in SAT scores was more a result of the expansion of the composition of students taking the test. This was due in large measure to the civil rights movement, which opened up opportunities for the poor.

A Nation at Risk galvanized the nation. Although it was but one of many reports on American education, it was couched in overheated prose at a time of renewed patriotic feeling. "If an unfriendly foreign power had attempted to impose on America the mediocre performance that exists today," the authors declared, "we might have viewed it as an act of war."[20] The media focused on American schooling in a feeding frenzy, and the excellence reform movement was in full swing. With President Reagan using his bully pulpit to espouse reform, the third major educational reform movement was under way.

What did *A Nation at Risk* and the excellence reformers propose as solutions to the ills of American education? They advocated a comprehensive series of recommendations that were essentially *cost-neutral*. Whereas the interventions of the equity reformers required additional services and money, the excellence reform movement had no price tag on it. This was another reason that conservatives such as Reagan felt comfortable in advocating excellence reform.

These cost-neutral recommendations were intended for raising national standards in the schools and reinstituting a core curriculum. Later, public school choice and vouchers were added to the list. Two of the most ardent excellence reformers, John E. Chubb and Terry M. Moe, presented the most comprehensive change of all: the abandonment of democratic education. In their 1990 book *Politics, Markets and American Schools*, Chubb and Moe argued that "democratic institutions by which American public education has been governed . . . appear to be incompatible with effective schooling."[21] Indeed, they proposed that "reformers would do well to entertain that choice *is* a panacea. It has the capacity *all by itself* to bring about the kind of transformation that, for years, reformers have been seeking to engineer in myriad other ways."[22] By "choice" they meant vouchers for private and parochial schools. Indeed, neoconservative historian Diane Ravitch would now advocate, as assistant secretary of education in the Bush administration, a core curriculum that was reflective mostly of the Western tradition. In lieu of that, she opted for school choice of the voucher variety as promoted by Chubb and Moe, since she felt that "we have . . . no reason to support public education."[23]

Continuing cost-neutral programs in excellence reform, President George Bush announced six national educational goals, which, for the most part did not require infusions of federal monies. These included a high school graduation rate of 90 percent; students in fourth, eighth, and twelfth grades to be competent in the five basic subjects; students to be first in math and science. These Bush goals, that required money, were that all children would be ready for school; all adults would be literate; and all schools would be free of drugs. President Bush mainly increased funding for the Head Start preschool program for poor children after the twenty-year longitudinal study on the Ypsilanti, Michigan, Head Start program had established the effectiveness of that approach.

President Bill Clinton adopted his predecessor's national educational goals but added three more. These included professional development for teachers; involvement of parents in school partnership; and the objective of safe schools free from violence. The last had a notable price tag. The 1993 Gun Free School Act provides funds for innovative programs to reduce school violence.

Along with the national goals, Bush initiated the development of national standards for the main subject areas. Bush declared that excellence reform was essentially cost-neutral. At the Education Summit he called in Charlottesville, Virginia, in the fall of 1989, he told the nation's governors that "Our focus must be no longer on our resource but must be on results."[24] His chief of staff, John Sununu, echoed Bush by declaring that, as far as the schools were concerned "money . . . therefore was not the problem."[25] Moreover, Bush advocated a choice plan that would include private and parochial schools.

The Bush goals and standards were attacked by equity reformers. They argued that raising standards would adversely affect at-risk (read: poor and minority) students. Typical of the responses was that of the assistant commissioner of education in New York, Lester W. Young Jr. His appraisal indicated that higher standards without monied programs "will create large numbers of students at risk."[26]

SOCIAL SCIENCE AND EDUCATIONAL POLICY

During the course of the excellence reform movement, conflicting evidence about the relationship of school finance emerged from educational researchers. First came testimony that key Great Society programs, such as Head Start, were uncommonly effective. Later, a meta-analysis of numerable studies on the relationship between money and student performance concluded that money had little to do with school improvement. Equity reformers focused on the Head Start data, whereas excellence reformers were anxious to show that the key was raising standards and restructuring schools rather than pouring more dollars into the ailing American school system.

The first Head Start study in 1969, conducted by the Westinghouse Learning Corporation and Ohio University, concluded that the four-year-old preschool program was "extremely weak."[27] The researchers found no difference in academic achievement between Head Start preschoolers and non-Head Start preschoolers. However, the crucial research that changed opinion on Head Start programs was released in 1984. One study reviewing Head Start programs published in 1978 indicated positive effects.[28] A twenty-year longitudinal evaluation of the Perry Preschool Program in Ypsilanti, Michigan, offered dramatic evidence on the efficacy of properly implemented Head Start programs. Longitudinal studies yield robust data by following a group's educational progress over a long period of time. However, such an approach is limited, since only a small sample can be tracked. In the Perry study, 123 poor black youths were followed from preschool to the age of nineteen and a work environment. The researchers found that the Perry youngsters achieved better than a control group without a preschool program. The Perry youngsters performed better academically, had less of a dropout rate, and had an employment and college attendance rate double that of their control counterparts. The researchers considered the implication adding a cost-benefit analysis.

These benefits considered in terms of their economic value make the preschool program a worthwhile investment for society. Over the lifetimes of the participants, preschool is estimated to yield economic benefits with an estimated value that is over seven times the cost of one year of the program.[29]

In response to the Perry study, President Bush proposed a 20 percent increase in Head Start funding.[30]

Excellence reformers received a boost in their cost-neutral approach from a 1989 meta-analysis of 187 qualified studies on the relationship of expenditure to student achievement. Meta-analysis is a recently popular research methodology whereby a group of statistical studies on a particular topic are refactored to establish a trend. In his meta-analysis on "the impact of differential expenditures on school expenditures," Eric Hanusek concluded that *"there is no strong or systematic relationship between school expenditures and student performance."*[31] Hanusek reviewed studies on school finance and student achievement that used a production model, factoring quantitative inputs such as family background, teacher characteristics, and instructional expenditures to the outputs of standardized tests. The production model was first used by James Coleman et al. in the massive 1964 U.S. Department of Education study, *Equality of Educational Opportunity*. Commonly known as the Coleman Report, the study was the first to conclude that school resources had little input on student achievement. Coleman argued that the most important variable was family background. Hanusek's meta-analysis reaffirmed Coleman's thesis.

The school research of the 1970s by such scholars as Michael Rutter and Wilbur Brookover successfully challenged the Coleman thesis of family background. In their studies, Rutter and Brookover, and others using both quantitative and ethnographic methodologies, found that children from lower socioeconomic backgrounds could achieve academically, provided that a school possessed a strong positive climate and such qualitative variables as a principal who acted as an *educational* leader, teachers with high expectations of students, rigorous classroom work schedules, and parent participation. Excellence reformers quickly perceived that these variables were, for the most part, cost-neutral. Consequently, Chester E. Finn, Jr., assistant secretary for research in the Reagan Administration, championed effective school research in his publication of *What Works* for teachers and principals.

Equity reformers were not on the defensive. Secretary of Education Lamar Alexander in the Bush administration declare on such popular venues as the television commentary *The McNeil Lehrer News Hour* that research (read: Hanusek's meta-analysis) now proved that money had little influence on the academic achievement of students. In the academic journals, far removed from the mass media, meta-analysis had its critics. They argued that a major problem with the technique is that meta-analysis may be difficult to interpret due to the complexities of the differing statistical methods employed in the various studies. Consequently, the result would be chimeric.

Some scholars reanalyzed Hanusek's meta-analysis and concluded the opposite. Larry V. Hedges, Richard D. Laine, and Rob Greenwald published their revision of Hanusek in 1994 in the *Educational Researcher*, the same scholarly publication that five years earlier published Hanusek's meta-analysis. In reviewing Hanusek's statistical analysis they concluded that:

Reanalysis with more powerful analytic methods suggests strong support for at least some positive effects of resource inputs and little support for the existence of negative effects.[32]

Researchers also assailed choice as "a silver bullet" that offers "a cheap path to educational reform."[33] In 1992, the Carnegie Foundation for the Advancement of Teaching published its study of choice programs. The foundation researchers found a "mixed report card," with some programs achieving educational gains among students.[34] However, they added that "it seems clear that other factors besides choice have been involved."[35] One of the main "other factors" was money. "In every district-wide program we examined," the researchers declared, "significant additional administrative and financial support has been crucial."[36]

A case in point has been the much-heralded District 4 choice program in East Harlem, New York City. Promoted by Principal Deborah Meier, who was to achieve national prominence and designation as a MacArthur Foundation "genius," choice depended much on an infusion of federal funds. From the 1970s to the mid-1980s, District 4 received "more federal money per student than any in the nation."[37] With the addition of thirty teachers, test scores of students increased. From 1988 to 1992, both federal, state, and local monies dropped under tight budget constraints, and the test scores of District 4 students concomitantly dropped,[38] The Carnegie researchers concluded that "choice is not enough."[39]

POST-EXCELLENCE REFORM

Two developments indicated that excellence reform was fading. First, many excellent reformers were losing faith in restructuring public education and advocated privatization—American business running public schools for profit. Second, a conservative sweep in the November 1994 Congressional and gubernatorial elections signified a redirected national focus from education to the social issues of crime, welfare, and immigration.

In 1991, Education Alternatives, Inc., contracted out in several public school systems to manage the academic and school plant functions. EAI was able to secure assignments for pilot programs in Baltimore, Los Angeles, and Miami-Dade County, and for the entire school system of Hartford, Connecticut. Not far behind AEI, Chris Whittle, a market salesman, was able to launch a more heralded privatization effort, titled The Edison Project. Whittle secured the services of excellence reformers John Chubb on his seven-member design team. Chester Finn, Jr., one of the most visible champions of excellence reformers, was as a consultant. The Edison Project slowly gathered contracts with public school systems.

The argument of privatization advocates was that American public schools were in need of the entrepreneurial skills of business in order to succeed academically, with the greatest efficiency and the least cost. Early evaluations of EAI's programs in Baltimore and Miami indicated that the privatization failed to live up to its advance notices. Students in the Miami schools did not do better than counterparts, and the contract was not renewed. In Baltimore, the nine schools under EAI also did not improve in test scores. Most important, in Baltimore, EAI received $18 million more in funds for their "experiment."[40] In short, privatization was the most radical comprehensive change to appear in recent years, and it reflected the exhaustion of excellence reform ideas.

Equally important, the conservative electoral sweep in the fall of 1994 was a benchmark of the decline of excellence reform. In every state, polls revealed that the major issues which concerned the American public were crime, welfare, and immigration. Education was falling as a major concern. This is to be compared with education as the second most important issue in voters' minds in 1984 after *A Nation at Risk*. Moreover, the Republican conservatives resurrected as their educational agenda one identical to that of Ronald Reagan prior to *A Nation at Risk*, namely, school prayer, vouchers, and the elimination of the U.S. Department of Education. The "new" conservative agenda constituted a backward step.

What are we to conclude about the politics of educational reform in our history? First, major educational reform is the result of outside societal forces. Second, there is a penchant for both comprehensive change and innovation. Third, American presidents became more involved in educational reform, setting a national agenda after World War II when the nation became the dominant technological society in the world.

NOTES

1. E.D. Hirsch, Jr., *Cultural Literacy* (New York: Houghton Mifflin, 1987), p. xvii.

2. Ibid.

3. Diane Ravitch, *The Troubled Crusade* (New York: Basic Books, 1983), p. 255.

4. William Julius Wilson, *The Truly Disadvantaged* (Chicago: University of Chicago Press, 1987), pp. 34–35.

5. Ravitch, *The Troubled Crusade*, p. 237.

6. Ibid., p. 260.

7. Ibid., p. 261.

8. U.S. Department of Education, *America 2000: An Education Strategy* (Washington, D.C.: U.S. Government Printing Office, April 18, 1990), pp. 16–178.

9. Jerome Bruner, *The Process of Education* (New York: Vintage Books, 1960), p. 33.

10. Nelson F. Ashline et al., *Education, Inequality and National Policy* (Lexington, Massachusetts: Lexington Books, 1976), p. xviii.

11. Charles Dean McCoy, *The Education President* (Austin: University of Texas Press, 1975), p. 74.

12. Lyndon B. Johnson, "The Goals: Ann Arbor," in *The Great Society Reader*, ed. Marvin E. Gettelman and David Mermelstein (New York: Random House, 1967), p. 15.

13. George Reedy, *Lyndon B. Johnson: A Memoir* (New York: Andrews and McNeel, 1982), p. 22.

14. E. Edmund Reutter, Jr., and Robert R. Hamilton, eds., *The Law of Public Education*, 2nd ed. (Mineola, New York: Foundation Press, 1976), p. 220.

15. Benjamin M. Friedman, *Day of Reckoning* (New York: Random House, 1988), p. 19.

16. Lester C. Thurow, *The Zero-Sum Society* (New York: Penguin Books, 1981), p. 5.

17. Terrell H. Bell, *The Thirteenth Man: A Reagan Cabinet Memoir* (New York: Free Press, 1988), p. 22.

18. U.S. Department of Education, "Responses to Reports from the Schools,"

in *The Great School Debate*, ed. Beatrice and Ronald Gross (New York: Simon and Schuster, 1985), p. 392.

19. National Commission on Excellence in Education, *A Nation at Risk: The Imperative for Educational Reform* (Washington, D.C.: U.S. Department of Education, 1983), p. 5.

20. Ibid., p. 5.

21. John E. Chubb and Terry M. Moe, *Politics, Markets and American Schools* (Washington, D.C.: The Brookings Institute, 1990), p. 2.

22. Ibid., p. 216.

23. Diane Ravitch, "Multiculturalism: E Pluribus Unum," in Paul Berman, ed., *Debating P.C.* (New York: Laurel, 1992), p. 296.

24. George Bush, "Remarks by the President," The White House Office of the Press Secretary, Charlottesville, Virginia, September 28, 1989, p. 5.

25. Tom Wicker, "Bush's Report Card," *New York Times*, October 6, 1989, p. A31.

26. *New York Times*, December 6, 1989, p. 14.

27. Maurice R. Berube, "Head Start to Nowhere," *Commonweal*, May 30, 1969, p. 311.

28. Irving Lazar and Richard B. Darlington, *Lasting Effects After Preschool* (Ithaca, New York: Cornell University Press, October, 1978), p. 2.

29. John R. Berrueta-Clement et al., *Changed Lives: The Effect of the Perry Preschool Program on Youths Through Age 19* (Ypsilanti, Michigan: The High Scope Press, 1989), p. 1.

30. George Bush, "Address to Congress," *New York Times*, February 10, 1989, p. A17.

31. Eric A. Hanusek, "The Impact of Differential Expenditures on School Performance," *Educational Researcher*, May, 1989, p. 47.

32. Larry V. Hedges, Richard D. Laine, and Rob Greenwald, "Does Money Matter? A Meta-Analysis of Studies of the Effects of Differential School Inputs on Student Outcomes," *Educational Researcher*, April, 1994, p. 13.

33. The Carnegie Foundation for the Advancement of Teaching, *School Choice* (Princeton, New Jersey: The Carnegie Foundation for the Advancement for Teaching, 1992), p. 23.

34. Ibid.

35. Ibid.

36. Ibid.

37. Ibid., p. 42.

38. Ibid.

39. Ibid., p. 21.

40. Albert Shanker, "What Are They Selling?" *New York Times*, June 25, 1995, p. E7.

5

The Politics of National Standards

Public education in the United States is essentially a political enterprise. The content and administration of public schooling are dependent on citizen tax dollars determined by elected city and state officials and on policies fashioned by elected school boards and appointed state officials. Unfortunately, the politics of education is mostly ignored by educators, parents, students—and the general public. Our educational body politic suffers from tunnel vision. We consider educational ideas, programs, and reform movements mainly from a conceptual basis with no other societal links. In short, for many educators it is a case of education for education's sake.

The excellence reform movement that erupted on the national scene more than a decade ago with the U.S. Department of Education's study *A Nation at Risk: The Imperative for Educational Reform* was the result of international politics. As the American economy declined in the face of strong foreign competition, most notably from Japan, a simple solution was sought to resolve a complex economic problem. What was at fault, critics maintained, was a mediocre public school system that short-changed America's scientific brainpower to produce consumer goods. Left out of this rush to judgment were poor business decisions, a bloated military complex that drained at least half of our scientists—among our best—for defense and space industries, and a declining work ethic in the general populace in the aftermath of thirty years (1945–75) of enormous affluence.

The main advocates for excellence reform were, as David Cohen has noted, educational "professionals and politicians."[1] Our educational history suggests that the educational community is obsessed with innovation and change. Consequently, many educators are at the ready for the newest reform bandwagon. As for politicians, it is much easier to influence school reform than the corporate world and the work motivation of the general public.

What this unlikely alliance of educators and politicians proposed was to revamp public schools by making education more rigorous. The cry was to raise standards so that Johnny would compare more favorably in international tests with Hiro or Dieter. Never mind that when the international testing samples were controlled, Johnny did as well or better. Excellence reform was a major national issue for over a decade. Business became active, and the media kept educational reform before the general public. However, the excellence school reform movement received a near-fatal shock in the November 1994 congressional sweep by ultraconservatives. Although excellence reform was championed by no fewer than three presidents—Ronald Reagan, George Bush, and Bill Clinton—it is fading as a national issue. Responding to the polls, voters put educational reform aside and concentrated on crime, welfare, and immigration issues. Indeed, conservative politicians have revived President Reagan's pre-*A Nation at Risk* educational policy by advocating school prayer, vouchers for private and parochial schools, and the elimination of the U.S. Department of Education. The issue of national standards is a last gasp of the excellence reform movement, caught between two changing political worlds.

The irony is that the nation has adopted the idea of national standards at a time when the excellence reform movement is fading as a national priority. Forty-nine states are developing standards for their public schools, with Iowa the sole holdout. For their many advocates, national standards have become an "astonishingly ambitious" effort that is the "fruit of nearly a decade's efforts to dramatically transform American education."[2]

The national standards movement reveals the essential weakness of excellence reform. Raising standards and providing public and/or private school choice programs are cost-neutral approaches that promise easy and quick solutions to an enormously complicated schooling process. For one thing, as equality reformers of the 1960s pointed out, raising standards will most likely cause more at-risk students (read: "poor and minority") to fail without large infusions of money for intervention programs. Yet none of the proponents of national standards addresses the issue of at-risk students and cost.

Equally important, the national standards movement is a throwback to the rote memorization era that preceded the progressive education revolution of the turn of the century. By emphasizing that content standards be measured by a system of voluntary testing, excellence reformers have shed the critical-thinking, problem-solving character that John Dewey and his colleagues made a distinctive feature of American education. At a time when our European and Eastern national counterparts envy our emphasis on developing thinking skills, American excellence reformers are disavowing that progressive contribution. In his best-selling book *Cultural Literacy*, which became the bible of the standards movement, E.D. Hirsch Jr., renounced Dewey and progressive ideas. Hirsch called Dewey "the writer who has most deeply affected American educational history and practice," whose advocacy of "the content-neutral curriculum . . . was deeply mistaken."[3]

Eliot Eisner has criticized the national standards movement as a "well-intentioned but conceptually shallow effort to improve our schools" that betrays the unique function of American education.[4] According to Eisner, what we need to teach is not content-specific curricula but "how to engage in higher-order thinking, how to pose telling questions, how to solve complex problems that have more than one answer."[5]

The truth of the matter is that most of the advocates of excellence reform are political conservatives. In the other two great educational reform movements—the progressive education reform movement and the equity reform movement of the 1960s—the chief activists were either liberals or radicals. One can understand why those equity reformers that are still active today—such as Marilyn Gittell and Stanley Aronowitz, who are more concerned with the poor and disenfranchised—should be suspicious of excellence reform and national standards. Even mainstream critics such as Eisner are wary of the direction and content of national standards.

In addition to the intellectual and scholarly opposition from the left, there is a major threat to national standards and excellence reform from ultraconservatives who have captured national and state gubernatorial offices. Since the Great Society of the 1960s, the American public has progressively moved to the right. So the neoconservative advocates of national standards, such as Albert Shanker of the American Federation of Teachers and Chester E. Finn Jr., assistant secretary of education under Ronald Reagan, see their reform movement threatened by colleagues from within their own camp.

The political battle for national standards has been on two fronts: the formulation of the standards and their implementation. Mary Bicouvaris in her essay on this issue in *The Clearing House* describes the infighting among members of the history standards panel. In seeking a consensus on standards, one must acknowledge the existence of deeply held political and educational views that span the spectrum from left to right. Standards in mathematics that were devised after a ten-year period by the National Council of Teachers of Mathematics in 1989 were atypical of the standards process. Numbers have no social, political, or moral context.

Not so with such a volatile subject as American history. The standards settled on were strongly buffered by political winds. Senator Joseph McCarthy was mentioned nineteen times, whereas Albert Einstein, Robert E. Lee, and the Wright brothers were ignored. Most troubling to the religious right was the omission of the Constitution's declaration that the nation has a Creator.[6] The debate spilled over into the U.S. Senate. On January 18, 1995, the Senate passed a resolution by a vote of ninety-nine to one condemning the national standards in American history.

Advocates of national standards have eschewed the political battles that, inevitably, have taken place. Diane Ravitch, the neoconservative educational historian who served in the Bush administration as assistant secretary of education for research, exemplifies this mindset. In her 1995 book *National Standards in American Education: A Citizen's Guide*, Ravitch expressed concern over the politics of national standards: "I began the book as an advocate of a particular approach to the issues; as time went by, events changed my perceptions and my point of view. I continued to support strongly the idea of standards but had become deeply concerned about the problems of their implementation and the possibility of their politicization."[7]

Ravitch was being wary. In the first major confrontation over school curriculum guidelines, she took an extremely political and activist stance, criticizing the report of the 1989 New York State task force on a social studies curriculum for high school students, *A Curriculum of Inclusion*, as repeatedly expressing "negative judgments on European Americans and on everything Western and European."[8] Moreover, she authored a manifesto, "Statement of Committee of Scholars in Defense of History" signed by twenty-six other historians, to condemn *A Curriculum of Inclusion*.

Moreover, the GOALS 2000 legislation sought to have the formulation of national standards developed and monitored by the National Education Standards and Improvement Council (NESIC). However, as David Cohen pointed out, "NESIC seems dead on arrival" because the new conservatives elected in the November 1994 congressional elections "had little use for any sort of national school reform . . . [and] especially little use for an agency that would devise, promulgate, and certify national educational standards."[9] Without NESIC, the standards movement, according to Howard Gardner, "may fall apart, like a crumbling Babel, or . . . it may end up by crippling some of the most promising reform efforts underway in our country."[10]

The purpose of national standards is to increase learning. That is the bottom line. Ravitch lists as her first argument in her "case for national standards" that "standards can improve achievement by clearly defining what is to be taught and what kind of performance is to be expected."[11] But standards advocates are quick to admit that, as Ravitch concedes, national standards "will accomplish little by themselves."[12] They must be linked, as David Cohen suggests, to "thoughtful school improvement strategies that include standards."[13] Unfortunately, these excellence reformers have seriously misread the history of school reform in this country. Very little school reform has been meaningful without adequate funding. Excellence reform and national standards, however, have been sold to the American public as cost-neutral reforms that are essentially free to the taxpayer.

There is a larger political current that may doom the national standards movement. As noted, educational reform is not a national priority with the new political forces setting the national domestic social agenda in Washington. Does that mean that public education will stagnate? Not necessarily. Our educational history suggests that educators are obsessed with innovation, guaranteeing piecemeal change at the local level. But the American public has spoken. As a national movement, excellence reform appears dead. It had an unexpectedly long life.

NOTES

1. David Cohen, "What Standards for National Standards?" *Phi Delta Kappan*, June, 1995, pp. 751–57.
2. Ibid., p. 751.
3. E.D. Hirsch, Jr., *Cultural Literacy* (New York: Houghton Mifflin, 1987), p. xvii.
4. Eliot N. Eisner, "Standards for American Schools: Help or Hindrance?" *Phi Delta Kappan*, June, 1995, pp. 758–64.
5. Ibid., p. 763.
6. Anne E. Lewis, "An Overview of the Standards Movement," *Phi Delta Kappan*, June, 1995, pp. 745–50.
7. Diane Ravitch, *National Standards in American Education: A Citizen's Guide* (Washington, D.C.: The Brookings Institute, 1995), pp. xii–xiii.
8. Diane Ravitch, "Multiculturalism: E Pluribus Unum," in Paul Berman, ed., *Debating P.C.* (New York: Laurel, 1992), pp. 291–92.
9. David Cohen, "What Standards for National Standards?" p. 752.
10. Howard Gardner, "The Need for Anti-Babel Standards," *Education Week*, September 7, 1994, p. 56.
11. Diane Ravitch, *National Standards in Education*, p. 25.
12. Ibid., p. 24.
13. David Cohen, "What Standards for National Standards?" p. 754.

6

The Post-Millennium Blues: Is It "The End of Knowledge," Too?

As the last millennium ended, many reputable scholars had dismissed their fields of inquiry as having reached their end. Notices went out that it was "the end of art," "the end of science," and "the end of history." Many knowledgeable—and unknowledgeable—critics simply ignored the messages of these Cassandras.

I am not so sure that we have not also reached "the end of education." There are many signs that we have accumulated enough knowledge about teaching and learning that we have little to look forward to that is truly new and mind-sweeping in educational research.

I came to that conclusion a few years back when I finished a book I was writing at the time, *American School Reform: Progressive, Equity, and Excellence Movements, 1883–1993* (Greenwood, 1994). It seemed to me, looking over the history of American education, that there were three great school reform movements, and that there was unlikely to be another. There would be innovation, yes, but nothing approaching the grand scale of these three major movements.

I was also bolstered in my thinking about "the end of education" by a provocative meta-analysis (a sophisticated review of the literature in one area) that was published in the *Review of Education Research* in the fall of 1993. The authors, Margaret C. Wang, Geneva D. Hartel, and Herbert J. Walberg, had reviewed an enormous body of studies on teaching and learning. In writing this mother of all meta-analyses, they found a knowledge base "distilled from an enormous body of knowledge extending over the last half-century" that constitutes "a reasonable basis for formulating educational policies and practices."[1] In short, we know all that essentially needs to be known about knowing.

As an educational historian, I shared certain assumptions about the nature of history with my academic colleagues in art, science, and history. In a word, we are all disciples of Thomas Kuhn (*The Structure of Scientific Revolution*, University of Chicago Press, 1962), which means that we view history in terms of paradigms, "big bang" shifts in the development of humankind. We do not approach our particular discipline of history in linear fashion, with incremental progress as an inevitable process.

What we Kuhnites are saying is that the major discoveries have been made in our areas. What is left to discover is important, but minor. We have reached the end.

Consider the art critic Arthur Danto's provocative essay "The End of Art." "The history of art has no future," Danto argues, "against the paradigms of progress, it sunders into a sequence of individual acts, one after another."[2] After abstract expressionism and pop art, he believes, there will be no other major art movements. "There is no longer any reason to think of art as having a progressive history," Danto concludes.[3] "The age of pluralism" is what remains. Art has reached its final paradigm shift.

Likewise, John Horgan in *The End of Science* posits that "science may be ending because it worked so well."[4] The only major discovery remaining is the unified-field theory in physics, a Holy Grail that eluded Albert Einstein for the last thirty years of his life.

What "discoveries" remain would be minor, what Horgan calls "ironic science."[5] Ironic science would not be the kind of Newton, Darwin, or Einstein. Ironic science, Horgan contends, cannot give us "the answer."[6]

Finally, we confront the end of political history. In his essay "The End of History?" later expanded into a book (*The National Interest*, 1989), Francis Fukuyama contends that the end of the cold war brought the major political movements to an end. Between the struggle of fascism, communism, and democracy, the end of the cold war marked a "triumph of the West, of the Western idea."[7]

What happened was "very fundamental," Mr. Fukuyama argues, so that there occurred "the total exhaustion of viable systematic alternatives in Western liberalism."[8] In the wake of the end of history, we are faced not with global conflict but smaller regional, religious, and national confrontations.

Could we Kuhnites—and Kuhn himself—be wrong? If the historical law of paradigms truly exists, we cannot foresee major turning points. Some leading educators have already accepted the fact that we are at the end of knowledge. The eminent educator John I. Goodlad has written that "we have an incredible body of knowledge."[9] The late teacher-educator Madeline Hunter was quoted as saying that "we now know enough about teaching."[10] Even former U.S. Secretary of Education William J. Bennett declared that teaching and learning is no longer "mysterious," and that "discovering what works has been a signal achievement of the reform movement to date."[11]

What we may be left with is nostalgia for a time when the struggle to know was still in doubt. Mr. Fukuyama has admitted that for him "the end of history" is a "sad time," occasioning a "powerful nostalgia for the time when history existed."[12]

It is the beginning of the post-millennium blues.

NOTES

1. Margaret C. Wang, Geneva D. Hartel, and Herbert J. Walberg, "Toward a Knowledge Base for School Learning," *Review of Educational Research*," Fall, 1993, p. 280.

2. Arthur Danto, "The End of Art," in *The Death of Art*, Berel Lang, ed. (New York: Haven, 1984), p. 24.

3. Ibid.

4. John Horgan, *The End of Science* (New York: Addison-Wesley, 1996), p. 9.

5. Ibid., p. 8.

6. Ibid.

7. Francis Fukuyama, "The End of History?" *The National Interest*, Summer, 1989, p. 3.

8. Ibid.

9. John I. Goodlad, "The Vision Thing: Educational Research and AERA in the 21st Century, Part 2," *Educational Researcher*, June/July, 1997, p. 13.

10. Madeline Hunter in Dwight Allen's Television Course, "Educational Reform," Old Dominion University, Norfolk, Virginia, April 10, 1988.

11. William J. Bennett, *American Education: Making it Work* (Washington, D.C.: U.S. Department of Education, April, 1988), p. 1.

12. Francis Fukuyama, "The End of History?" p. 18.

7

A Teacher's Legacy

Given today's critical climate in education, one welcomes the occasional tribute to a teacher. That is why the recent revival of interest in the writings of French Nobel laureate Albert Camus should come as welcome news to classroom teachers. One could argue that, in the history of the field, few teacher-pupil relationships have had more dramatic impact than that of Louis Germain on his young pupil Albert Camus.

Camus's work as a novelist, playwright, and philosopher has been part of the Western canon for over half a century. *The Stranger* is one of the most widely read novels of our time, and the philosophical essays *The Rebel* and *The Myth of Sisyphus* continue to be read.

With the 1996 publication of *The First Man*, his unfinished autobiographical novel, the French master reveals years after his death the debt he owed to his public elementary schoolteacher. Camus's daughters decided to publish *The First Man* in the belief that it would be of exceptional value to those interested in Camus's life.

We are apprised in the foreword that "once you have read *The First Man* you will understand why the appendix includes the letter Albert Camus wrote to his teacher, Louis Germain, after receiving the Nobel Prize, and the last letter Louis Germain wrote to him. Little is known about Louis Germain save for the warm portrait of him in *The First Man*.

This autobiographical novel recounts the classic story of a poor boy who made good. Camus was born and raised in Algeria in a female-headed household. His father died in World War I, when Camus was no more than a year old. Camus's mother was partially deaf, his uncle totally so, and his grandmother dominated a household that also included Albert's slightly older brother. The parental figures could neither read nor write. The grandmother's intention was that the young Camus would help relieve the family's bitter poverty by apprenticing to a local tradesman.

But Camus was precocious, and school became a sanctuary for him where he could "escape family life." What he and his classmates "so passionately loved in school," according to the book, "was that they were not at home, where want and ignorance made life harder and more bleak."

Camus became his teacher's pet. And Louis Germain's influence on the boy was crucial in switching the tracks on his prescribed destiny. It is a familiar story which I have found repeated often in my investigations of educating poor children. The teacher often becomes the main actor, rather than the parents.

Here is what Albert Camus, fresh from his speech in Stockholm accepting the Nobel Prize for literature, had to say to his former teacher:

Dear Monsieur Germain,

I let the commotion around me these days subside a bit before speaking to you from the bottom of my heart. I have just been given far too great an honor, one I neither sought nor solicited. But when I heard the news, my first thought, after my mother, was of you. Without you, without the affectionate hand you extended to the small poor child that I was, without your teaching, and your example, none of all this would have happened. I don't make too much of this sort of honor. But at least it gives me an opportunity to tell you what you have been and still are for me, and to assure you that your efforts, your work, and the generous heart you put into it still live in one of your little schoolboys who, despite the years, has never stopped being your grateful pupil. I embrace you with all my heart:

—Albert Camus[1]

A copy of this letter should be kept in every teacher's desk.

NOTE

1. Albert Camus, *The First Man* (New York: Vintage Books, 1996), p. 321.

PART III

CULTURE

8

Arts and Education

Americans first matured culturally after World War II. The affluence brought on by technological developments maintained the economic dominance that the United States had achieved in the late 1800s as a manufacturing nation. Moreover, the aftermath of war witnessed the rise of mass education with the GI Bill of Rights, which enabled nearly 2.5 million veterans to get a college education. Affluence and rising levels of education created conditions ripe for a culturally conscious society.

Correspondingly, the period saw a cultural renaissance. Abstract expressionism shifted the locus of international art from Paris to New York. The introductions of the quality paperback made literature and scholarship easily available to all of the educated public. American jazz and American serious music were receiving critical recognition.

This cultural boom went into high gear by 1975. The number of artists in all fields more than doubled between 1970 and 1990 to a high of 1,671,000 (Larson 1997). Museums also grew by 50 percent, totaling 1,200 with some 100 million visitors in 1996 (*New York Times* 1997b). Indeed, one observer noted that the art museum had become a social center— part "classroom, meeting place, restaurant, playground, park bench, party palace, cinema, singles bar, conversation provocateur, travel agent, lecture hall, wine bar . . . and . . . the place to see and be seen socially" (*New York Times* 1997b). A cultural elite emerged in America of people who are for the most part well educated and economically well off.

Yet two distinct American societies have developed: one that is culture conscious and one that is not. Indeed, the $7.3 billion spent on nonprofit art institutions represents only .133 percent of the gross national product (Larson 1997). Approximately 39 percent of Americans participate in sporting events and 37 percent are spectators (these figures may overlap some) (Larson 1997). By comparison, only 4 percent of adult Americans play classical music, 10 percent paint, 12 percent are fine arts photographers, 8 percent are involved in modern dance, and 7 percent engage in creative writing (Larson 1997). A recent survey indicated that the painter most admired by Americans is Norman Rockwell, considered by art critics not a painter at all but an illustrator. The least liked of nine international artists also listed in the survey was Jackson Pollock, with a rating of 4 percent compared to Rockwell's 43 percent. Pollock was not only America's greatest painter, but arguably the greatest painter of the twentieth century (Melamida et al. 1994).

There exists in America a strong anti-intellectual tradition, which was ably chronicled by the historian Richard Hofstadter some forty years ago in his book *Anti-Intellectualism in America*. In the late 1980s, no less than a vice president of the United States condemned the "cultural elite" who, allegedly, were undermining American family values. In the 1992 presidential election, both candidates, George Bush and Bill Clinton, dumbed themselves down for fear of alienating this public. They deliberately blurred their sophistication and their academic backgrounds at elite universities (Berube 1992).

On the other hand, the economic aspect of art is quickly being realized by politicians. A New York City economic impact study revealed that in the decade between 1982 and 1993, cultural tourism accounted for $9.2 billion in the New York City metropolitan area. Nonprofit institutions, including museums, theaters, and those that supported opera, music, and dance, among others, accounted for $2.7 billion. Art galleries and art auction houses had an impact of $848 million. Visitors to these cultural activities accounted for $2.3 billion spent on restaurants, hotels, airfare, shopping, taxis, and (30,000) additional jobs (Alliance for the Arts 1993).

This lesson in the economic impact of the arts has not been lost on museums and political figures in other cities. The Philadelphia Museum of Art held a much-heralded retrospective of Paul Cézanne in 1996 that was an enormous success. Tied in with the city's hotels, which offered an "art package," the exhibit drew some 750,000 visitors. A PBS television special features the Cézanne retrospective. The show's sponsors and the city of Philadelphia spent $3.4 million on advertising for the exhibit (*New York Times* 1996a). One indicator of the success of the Cézanne show was that the museum took in $17.5 million in admission and sales of art-related objects (Larson 1997). In addition, the city of Philadelphia received $122.6 million in tourist expenditures (Larson 1997). A museum official concluded that "cultural tourism really works" (*New York Times* 1996a. 3).

Other cities followed suit. Boston mounted a Picasso exhibition, with hotels also offering special packages. In 1996, the Norfolk-Virginia Beach area began an international arts festival featuring high art and low art and a combination of high art acts such as the Michael Morris ballet troupe and violinist Itzhak Perlman alongside a broadcast of Garrison Keillor's popular radio program, *A Prairie Home Companion*. As municipalities search for scarce dollars, cultural tourism is fast becoming a new player in town.

ARTS AND THE SCHOOLS

In the school, the role of arts in the curriculum has had a problematic history. The progressive education reformers at the turn of the century, led by John Dewey, held that education was composed of four main objectives—the development of a child's intellect, moral sense, social awareness, and aesthetic sense. Progressive education flourished in elite private schools serving an affluent constituency. Progressive educators pioneered in incorporating the arts into the school curricula. Still, the level of arts in the curriculum varied from school district to school district. But in 1957, with the launching of the Soviet missile Sputnik at the height of the cold war, a counterrevolution against progressive education took place: the public called for a return to "basic" in the schoolroom. The arts were the first part of the curriculum to be eliminated from many public schools. And the arts are still the first to be considered an educational frill to be discarded by budget cutters.

There was an attempt to return the arts to the curriculum during the Great Society of the 1960s. Money was provided in the historic 1965 Elementary and Secondary Education Act for arts programs, but these were merely "add-ons." The 1997 study, *American Canvas: An Arts Legacy for Our Communities* by the National Endowment for the Arts, concluded that "the arts do not have a secure place in the basic curriculum" (Larson 1997, 92).

Neither has the current excellence-in-education reform movement had a place for the arts in its standards and core curricula. For example, the 1983 document that ignited that movement, *A Nation at Risk: The Imperative for Educational Reform*, did not mention the arts in the core curricula, nor did President Bush's national goals in 1989.

The Clinton administration sought to place the arts in the National Standards Core Curricula along with English, history, math, science, and foreign languages. In 1994, voluntary standards on teaching in the arts were added to the core. Like the other standards, the arts standards are voluntary, which means that they will probably be last considered by government agencies and school systems operating under fiscal constraints.

The goals of these voluntary standards are for students to develop a knowledge base among the four arts disciplines—dance, music, theater, and the visual arts; to be able to "define and solve artistic problems" in at least one art form; and to be able to analyze works of art, have an understanding of great art, and relate knowledge across the arts disciplines (Larson 1997, 98). In short, the key concept is that of *understanding* the arts rather than being a practitioner.

The Clinton administration has budgeted $700 million for its national standards program. Some of this money would be directed by the states to arts curricula. The hope is that the states and localities will realize, according to a federal arts official, that "the arts are indispensable to education reform" (Larson 1997, 99).

Both the federal government and the foundations have provided financial incentives to public schools to involve students in art. In 1994, the federal government gave "seed" money of up to $40,000 to fifty museums on a one-year basis to design art education programs for public school students (*New York Times* 1997a). Foundations have provided most of the funds for such programs throughout the United States. For example, the Los Angeles County Museum received a $1 million grant from the Keck Foundation in addition to a $500,000 grant from the Irvine Foundation (*New York Times* 1997a).

These innovative programs seek to acquaint students with the treasures in museums, such as the Whitney Museum in New York City and the National Wildlife Art Museum in Jackson, Wyoming. In Washington, D.C., an imaginative art program for minority students called "Art Around the Corner" involves nearly 300 students from four schools. One day a month for a two-year period, the students go to school at the National Gallery of Art. The museum's staff visits the students at their schools as well. Such multiple-visit programs are "the most exciting and least known programs happening in education," according to the director of the Institute of Museum and Library Services (*New York Times* 1997a).

Museum officials consider these activities a means to build a future art constituency. Many have taken an extremely aggressive and proactive position in obtaining funds and recruiting the schools. Their only regret, according to one museum director, is that "most teachers got little in the way of art education . . . and . . . are intimidated by museums" (*New York Times* 1997a).

Arts curricula have been considered nonessential by school boards. With severe budget constraints on every governmental level, the result has been that half of all American schools have no full-time art teachers

(*New York Times* 1994). In the 15,000 school districts in America, there are only 114 art supervisors and 59 district art supervisors (Larson 1997). In 1991 in New York City, an arts-rich community, two-thirds of the public schools had no arts instruction (*New York Times* 1994). In 1998, one-third of elementary schools sampled nationally had no visual arts instruction or permanent art teacher (Herbert 1998).

But there has been a counterattack to the budget cutters. Consider New York City. When the city went bankrupt in the mid-1970s, some 14,000 teachers—most of them art and music teachers—lost their jobs. In 1992 the philanthropist Walter Annenberg earmarked $12 million of his $500 million gift to improve public education nationwide for arts programs in New York City—seed money to be matched by other private dona-tions. Correspondingly, New York City Mayor Rudolph Giuliani budg-eted $75 million over three years for arts and music instruction. Five hundred art and music teachers were hired in 1998 and 4,000 more were recruited for 1999. California is also seeking to restore the arts to the curriculum; to do so, the commissioner of education has submitted a $200 million budget proposal (*New York Times* 1998).

Another problem in the delivery of arts education is that so many demands are made on schools in poor areas that the arts are often the first to go. For example, in New York City, where school principals have to apply for arts money, those seeking the money are in middle-class neighborhoods, where students' standardized test scores tend to be sat-isfactory. In lower-class neighborhoods, where the test scores tend to be lower, principals often opt to emphasize the basics and exclude the arts entirely (*New York Times* May 1998).

What is the purpose of an arts curriculum? There is a correlation be-tween the arts and academic achievement in the basic subjects. More important, does art have a moral/spiritual component for those exposed to it? Does art make one a better person? Can it change a person? In 1996, the International Association of Educating Cities sponsored an in-ternational conference in Chicago, "The Arts and Humanities as Agents for Social Change," to address these weighty philosophical questions. Conference participants examined one hundred arts initiatives aimed at helping the disadvantaged—from a creative writing project for juveniles in jail to Internet arts programs for the poor. There was no consensus among artists and critics about art as a change agent. Robert Brustein, the critic and Yale drama teacher, even challenged the group to "name a single work of art that has ever changed anything" (*New York Times* 1996b).

Yet there are many who believe that the answer to the questions above is yes. John Dewey (1934) considered the art experience to be the highest form of spiritual and moral experience. "Art is more moral than the moralities," he wrote in his classic tome *Art as Experience* (348). Picasso claimed that art, by its very nature, is moral. Indeed, when one understands great art (which is one major purpose of an arts curriculum), one is moved by its spiritual values. Perhaps the final words belong to Jackson Pollock's lifelong artist friend, Reuben Kadish, who described the effect of one of Pollock's signature poured-all-over paintings:

One of the most important things about Pollock's work, actually, is that it isn't so much what you are looking at but it's what's happening to you looking at his particular work . . . It had a power and it changed your character and your personality. (Jackson Pollock 1987; emphasis added)

REFERENCES

Alliance for the Arts. 1993. *The Arts as an Industry: Their Economic Importance to the New York–New Jersey Metropolitan Region.* New York: Port Authority of New York and New Jersey.

Berube, M.R. 1992. "The Dumbing Down of the Candidates." *Virginian Pilot,* August 26, A12.

Dewey, J. 1934. *Art as Experience.* New York: Capricorn Books.

Herbert, D. 1998. "Model Approaches to Arts Education." *Principal,* March.

Jackson Pollock: Portrait of an Artist. 1987. Video. London: R.M. Arts.

Larson, E.O. 1997. *American Canvas: An Arts Legacy for Our Communities.* Washington, D.C.: National Endowment for the Arts.

Melamida, A. et al. 1994. "Painting by the Numbers: The Search for a People's Art." *The Nation,* March 14, 344.

New York Times. 1994. March 14, 139.

———. 1996a. Aug. 25, sec. 5, p. 3.

———. 1996b. Sept. 28, 15.

———. 1997a. Feb. 19, A22.

———. 1997b. Oct. 5, sec. 2, p. 1.

———. 1998. May 23, A14.

9

His Greatest Paintings Produce a "Spiritual Calm"—One That Jackson Pollock Was Never Able to Share

Jackson Pollock was America's finest painter. There is every reason to believe that he will rank with Picasso and Matisse (as he sometimes claimed he did) as one of the twentieth-century's greatest artists.

I am constantly making lists of people, dead or alive, whom I would want to meet or wish I had met. Jackson Pollock is always on the top of that list. I came to Greenwich Village during the summer of 1956—the same summer Pollock died—as a young graduate student at New York University. I patronized the Cedar Street Tavern, the legendary watering hole of the abstract expressionists, at Ninth Street and University Place (until it closed in 1963), and was fortunate to have had a passing acquaintance with several artists who gathered there, including Willem de Kooning and Franz Kline. Thus began my forty-two–year love affair with abstract expressionism.

The current retrospective of Pollock's work—the first in thirty years—at the Museum of Modern Art in New York City does much to reinforce the artist's reputation. It is the most comprehensive collection of his paintings and drawings ever shown, and includes such masterpieces as "Blue Poles: Number 11, 1952," which has not been seen in this country in 25 years. All of the great works are here, including "Autumn Rhythm," "Lavender Mist," "One (Number 31, 1950)." These giant canvases, hung in one room, sweep you into their world. Of course, many of Pollock's smaller "poured" or "dripped" works are there, too, along with a facsimile of his Long Island barn, where the artist developed his signature style by dripping house paint from worn-out brushes and sticks onto canvases spread over his studio floor.

A surprise for me was "Mural," the first major work Pollock created before embarking on his dripped painting. Peggy Guggenheim, who was an art dealer, had commissioned it in 1943 for her New York apartment. It was the largest work Pollock ever painted, and he had to knock out a wall in his apartment to make it. It's not as good as his great, poured masterpieces, but its size, colors, and repetitive images alone would have secured him a place in the history of art.

The poured paintings, in their complexity and color, produce a spiritual calm. That calm is what de Kooning first noticed about Pollock's drip technique. Pollock's artist friend Reuben Kadish remarked that these masterpieces have a "power to change your character and your personality."[1] In his review of the exhibition, Michael Kimmelman, an art critic for *The New York Times*, concluded that "Pollock's paintings remain the central story of modern art."[2]

Pollock was ridiculed in his lifetime. *Time* magazine called him Jack the Dripper, and *Life* profiled him in a condescending article with the title "Jackson Pollock: Is He the Greatest Living Painter in the United States?" He sold little in his lifetime, and died in a drunk-driving crash at the age of 44.

Today Pollock's reputation has soared in the art world but still suffers in the opinion of the general public. Four years ago, a survey on nine internationally known artists was conducted in the United States. Most admired by Americans was Norman Rockwell, whom 43 percent of those surveyed rated as their favorite painter (even though he really was an illustrator). Pollock was least liked, a favorite of only 4 percent.[3]

Nevertheless, Pollock's legend—a classic story of the tortured alcoholic artist—still captures the imagination. The actor Ed Harris told *The New York Times* he is developing a film, which he directed and starred in, based on the Pulitzer Prize-winning *Jackson Pollock: An American Saga* by Steven Naifeh and Gregory White Smith. Perhaps Harris was interested because he bears a slightly physical resemblance to the artist, and because Harris's best film roles have been those of surly, semi-articulate characters. "I guess I feel there are certain similarities between him and me, but he was more extreme than I've ever been," the actor said.[4] One expects the worst: Pollock's drinking and bad behavior as the core of the film. True, it is said that when Pollock was sober he was nearly mute, and when drunk often impossible—violent, insulting, and misogynistic.

But Pollock was more. He was a genius, despite his alcoholism. His friend de Kooning observed that when Pollock had been drinking he overcame his shyness and became a brilliant conversationalist.

In fact, his library at the time of his death reveals that Pollock was a deep and serious thinker. He owned the major works of his time in art, philosophy, theology, psychology, and world literature, including books by Freud, Jung, Adler; Joyce, Gide, Goethe, Camus, and Beckett among European novelists; and Melville, Fitzgerald, Faulkner, and Steinbeck among American. Darwin's *The Descent of Man* shared shelf space with Joseph Campbell's *Hero with a Thousand Faces*, and the magazines included such journals as *Partisan Review*, *Paris Review*, and *Modern Monthly*, a socialist publication. Pollock apparently did not possess any light or trashy fiction (which my daughter-in-law, a "postmodern" professor of English at a large midwestern university, finds deplorable).

Pollock's conversation seemed rather to be with the great masters. Along with his fellow abstract expressionists, he sought to produce an art that would transform American painting—which in the 1940s comprised "flowers, reclining nudes, and people playing the cello," according to the American painter Barnett Newman—and establish it as a dominant world force, equal to the work of the European masters.[5]

The abstract expressionists were highly intellectual and cultured, as one of them, the painter Robert Motherwell, constantly pointed out. Although for most, higher education consisted largely of art school, they were well read. Some, like Motherwell, Mark Rothko, and Ad Reinhardt, had attended elite universities. They created their own "street university" in the Village. The artists formed "the Club" in 1949, after *Life* had wondered, tongue in cheek, whether Pollock was the greatest living American painter. Every Friday night these artists—without alcohol— would listen to guest speakers give talks on art, philosophy, theology, music, and literature, and then engage in heated debates.

The debates continued at the Cedar Street Tavern. Norman Bluhm, a second-generation abstract expressionist, called the Cedar "the cathedral of American culture in the fifties."[6] Sometimes the cathedral got a bit raucous: Pollock's drunken escapades became the stuff of myth.

Of course, there was a price to pay for breaking the mold. Many of the abstract expressionists were suicidal. Some, like Arshile Gorky and Mark Rothko, took their lives; others, like the sculptor David Smith— and Jackson Pollock—died in acts of existential suicide, through drunken crashes. Others, like Franz Kline, simply drank themselves to death.

Their problems were both personal and professional. Once they had achieved their signature styles, most were unable to redefine themselves as the European masters, such as Matisse and Picasso, had done. The Americans had a single style, with innumerable variations on a theme. Kline complained that the art world "would not let me out of the harbor," that he was locked into his black-and-white calligraphic paintings.[7] A few, such as de Kooning, went on to have different artistic periods in a long life. Pollock, though, had reached an artistic dead end at the time of his death.

Howard Gardner, the psychologist and theorist of what he calls "multiple intelligences," ably described such risk-takers as Pollock: "Most innovators and most innovations are not well understood or appreciated at the time of their launching. The lives of the extraordinary are often rimmed with casualties, some psychological, some mortal . . . Most . . . have turned out to be difficult people—often tortured, inflicting suffering on those close to them."[8]

I know full well that meeting Pollock might have been a trying experience, perhaps one involving my humiliation. He was known to challenge newcomers with a metaphysical query "Who the hell are you?" in a voice thick with hostility. As his friend Kadish observed, one paid a price for knowing Pollock. But I would have paid it gladly. His friends loved him despite his giant faults. Another of his friends, the artist Milton Resnick, lamented: "Pollock made the world interesting. Of all the people I've known I wish most he was alive."[9]

POSTSCRIPT—*POLLOCK:* THE FILM

Pollock is the finest film of an artist ever made, and the most historically accurate. The story of Jackson Pollock, considered by many to be America's greatest painter, belongs to the genre of movies of tormented artists such as those about Michelangelo, Vincent van Gogh, Toulouse-Lautrec, and Pablo Picasso. But it surpasses these films in authenticity.

It's no wonder that *Pollock* has been praised by both film and art critics. Roger Ebert has included *Pollock* in his top-ten list of best movies of the year. The actor portraying Pollock, Ed Harris (who is also the director), and the actress portraying Pollock's wife Lee Krasner, Marcia Gay Harden, have been nominated for Academy Awards for best actor and best supporting actress. Stephen Holden, a *New York Times* film reviewer, called *Pollock* a "powerful biographical film."[10] Michael Kimmelman, the chief art critic for the *New York Times*, thought it "a gripping drama."[11] Moreover, Kimmelman wrote that "no other movie about an artist has been more respectful or respectable in pure art terms."[12]

Pollock was the artistic genius who skyrocketed across the American landscape (along with fellow abstract expressionists) to transform American painting into world-class work. His breakout work was a series of large, wall-sized poured paintings that are highly complex and lyrical. These masterpieces produce a spiritual calm, which his fellow artist Willem de Kooning first noted, and they are unmatched in the history of art.

By contrast, this breaker-of-the-mold's life was tortured. By all accounts Pollock was a complex, tormented individual. By age fifteen, he was well on the road to being an alcoholic. He was intelligent, well read in the serious literature of the day, but prone to bouts of violence and abusive behavior when drunk. As Reuben Kadish, a lifelong friend re-marked, there was a price to be paid for knowing Pollock. Yet some of his artist friends thought him an irreplaceable friend.

Sadly, Pollock died prematurely at age 44 in August 1956 in a drunken car crash on Long Island. As Kimmelman noted, Pollock "is the ideal artist for a movie, if there is such a thing."[13]

Pollock takes up in 1941, when the artist first met fellow artist Lee Krasner and both were part of the art colony in Greenwich Village. The movie closes with Pollock's death fifteen years later. The milestones of his career are dramatized.

While Pollock's life story is the stuff of myth, Ed Harris treats the man and the myth unsentimentally. He presents us with two intermingling stories: the rise of the great artist and the textured relationship with the artist's wife, Lee Krasner. Pollock was from the Midwest and Krasner from Brooklyn. Early on, Krasner perceived him to be the greatest artist in the Village and proceeded to nurse both him and his career. Marcia Gay Harden is a believable Krasner, assured and bold. The nuanced, often volatile, relationship between Pollock and Krasner could have stood alone as a story line.

Harris has the difficult task of giving us a credible Pollock. Harris does not quite fully inhabit Pollock, but his characterization still is the most persuasive of any attempted on film. Harris's enormous research helped him so that at times he does become Pollock, even though he has written that "I never wanted to pretend to be Pollock" and that he "wanted to be Ed Harris, using all the tools as an actor and performer to allow Pollock's experience to touch me, inspire me, lead me to an honest, true performance."[14]

And that it is. His performance and his film are authentic, a word used over and over again by Pollock and the abstract expressionists. Above all, these painters sought to be true to themselves as artists.

Harris had an advantage as a "method" actor. He had been an art student, and he took painting lessons during the course of the film. Kim-melman observes that "no actor has come vaguely as close to simulating a real painter painting as does Mr. Harris."[15] Moreover, Harris bears a strong physical resemblance to Pollock, and in some scenes one could not tell the difference between the two. (Harris gained thirty pounds to look more like the dissolute Pollock of the last years.)

Most important, Harris's film is true to the spirit of Jackson Pollock. There are minor inaccuracies, but they are not essential to the plot. Harris based his version on the Pulitzer Prize-winning 1989 biography of Pol-lock, *Jackson Pollock: An American Saga*, by Steven Naifeh and Gregory White Smith. It is a voluminous reference. Much of the dialogue in the script was actually spoken, although occasionally not by the actual per-son or in the correct context. For example, it was the artist-teacher Hans

Hoffman, and not Lee Krasner, who commented to Pollock that he should work from nature, to which Pollock gave his famous reply: "I am nature."[16] In other words, Pollock painted his subconscious.

Harris went to extreme lengths to make his film ring true. Pollock's farmhouse and barn in Long Island were featured, and while some notable settings were impossible to use, suitable substitutes were found. In place of Pollock's East Eighth Street apartment, which had been razed, a Tribeca location was used. As for the original Cedar Street Tavern, burned down in the mid-1960s, a similar old-time tavern in Brooklyn was used. (In the only extended scene at the Cedar with de Kooning—played by Val Kilmer—and Kline and Pollock, the setting seemed genuine. I was more sensitive to Kilmer's portrayal of de Kooning, who had a thick Dutch accent, but Kilmer was a plausible younger version of the master.)

Not being able to use original Pollock paintings was another limitation Harris faced, but he painted good faux Pollocks.

I could only detect one serious omission in the script: Pollock made his signature artistic breakthrough during a period of a few years in which he was sober. A great deal of credit for that sobriety was due to his new psychiatrist on Long Island. When he had exhausted his muse with the poured paintings, he could not reinvent himself as a painter. This occasioned the end of his sobriety at a time when his psychiatrist also died in an unrelated car crash.

The film is also flawed in making much of the celebrity of Pollock and not enough of the ridicule with which the general public regarded him. *Time* magazine laughingly called him Jack the Dripper, and *Life* made him the first art star with a mocking article: "Is He the Greatest Living American Painter?"

Now, there is no doubt that Jackson Pollock was one of the world's greatest painters. And even though Harris did not fully address the criticism Pollock received, he has made a film that is a benchmark by which to measure future film biographies of great painters.

NOTES

1. Reuben Kadish, *Jackson Pollock: Portrait of an Artist*, 1987, Video. London: R.M. Arts.

2. Michael Kimmelman, "How Even Pollock's Failures Enhance His Triumph," *New York Times*, October 30, 1998, p. E31.

3. A. Melamida et al., "Painting by the Numbers: The Search for a People's Art," *The Nation*, March 14, 1994, p. 344.

4. *New York Times*, December 11, 1998, p. E16.

5. Emile deAntonio, *Painters Painting*, New York: New Video, 1972.

6. Steven Naifeh and Gregory Smith, *Jackson Pollock: An American Saga* (New York: Clarkson N. Potter, 1989), p. 748.

7. April Kingsley, *The Turning Point: The Abstract Expressionists and the Transformation of American Art* (New York: Simon and Schuster, 1992), p. 313.

8. Howard Gardner, *Extraordinary Minds* (New York: Basic Books, 1997), p. 141.

9. Jeffrey Potter, *To a Violent Grave: An Oral Biography of Jackson Pollock* (New York: Pushcart Press, 1985), p. 280.

10. Stephen Holden, "Splashed Across Life's Canvas, Dripping," *New York Times*, September 30, 2000, p. B9.

11. Michael Kimmelman, "Frame by Frame, an Action Film Dripping with Art," *New York Times*, December 10, 2000, p. A15.

12. Ibid.

13. Ibid.

14. Ed Harris, "On Playing Pollock," in *Such Desperate Joy: Imagining Jackson Pollock*, ed. Helen A. Harrison (New York: Thunder's Mouth Press, 2001), p. xvi.

15. Kimmelman, "Frame by Frame, An Action Film Dripping with Art."

16. Reuben Kadish, *Jackson Pollock: Portrait of an Artist*, Video. London, R.M. Arts. 1987.

10

A Postmodern Jesus

The controversy over Terence McNally's play *Corpus Christi* provoked my interest in revisiting other literary alternative depictions of Jesus that departed from the conventional saccharine versions. *Corpus Christi* presents the Christ figure as an actively gay man.

In the conventional Sunday sermon Jesus has been traditionally presented as a visitor from another planet, heavenly blessed from birth, immune to normal human struggles. This Jesus is detached from the matrix of human history. He is a mild, placid man/god, and, as far as gods go, rather antiseptic. Jesus is ahistorical, a divine alien.

As a historian, I believe that historical figures as well as historical events must be viewed from multiple perspectives. There are no one-dimensional people or single interpretations of landmark events. With the emergence of scholarship on the historical Jesus, many theologians for the past generation have concentrated on the human aspect of Jesus' personhood rather than his divinity. So we now have occasion to broaden our concept of who Jesus was. But prior to the new theological history, a number of artists took license to speculate on some of Jesus' human dimensions and others continue to do so.

Of the "other Jesuses," I was most taken by Jules Dassin's fictional version of a Marxist Jesus. I first made contact with the Marxist Jesus over forty years ago as a young Catholic radical in New York fighting labor racketeering. I went to see a screening of Dassin's magnificent film

He Who Must Die at the Eighth Street Cinema in Greenwich Village. Dassin had been a Hollywood director who was identified as a Communist during the House Un-American Activities Committee's anti-Communist hysteria in the 1950s. He fled the United States for Europe and was blacklisted. Dassin adapted Greek poet Nikos Kazantzakis' novel, *The Greek Passion*, which dealt with the Christ story. In Dassin's hands, Christ became a political revolutionary.

He Who Must Die recycles the Christ story as a modern fable of a revolution of the poor and oppressed in Greece under the domination of affluent Turks shortly after World War I. Villagers are chosen to reenact the Passion Play. They are ordinary people: The Christ figure is a shepherd with a speech defect, Peter is a postman, Judas is a black man and a leather worker. Their participation in the play serves to ignite their resistance to the local priest who collaborates with the Turks. Eventually under the leadership of the Christ figure, the actors stage a revolutionary uprising. It is an abortive attempt with the Christ figure dying at the hands of the Turks. Unfortunately, *He Who Must Die* is yet to be released on video.

He Who Must Die received numerous awards in Communist countries. In the United States the film was also highly praised. *Time* magazine named it one of its "choice movies for 1958", hailing it as "one of the most powerful religious statements the screen has seen in many a year."[1] The *Time* reviewer considered Dassin "a broadly and intensely gifted artist, one of the best in the film business." *The New Yorker* reviewer, John McCarten, considered *He Who Must Die* "one of the best pictures of recent years."[2] McCarten felt that the "philosophical core" of the film was the "unhappy proposition that if Christ were to return today he would be as sorely tried as he was two-thousand years ago."[3]

Even Catholic liberals praised the film. Philip Hartung of *Commonweal* considered *He Who Must Die* "a fascinating and moving film," but one that is "quite complicated" and "will mean many things to many people."[4] Hartung conceded the possibility that the film could be interpreted as "an argument against organized religion." Yet he concluded that *He Who Must Die* "provides a thought-provoking and enriching experience."[5]

The reviewer for *The Nation*, Robert Hatch, understandably found the film to be an evocation of "unstressed profundity" which Dassin "brought beautifully to the screen" with "the simplicity of real elegance."[6] Hatch singled out Dassin's "courage to deal with moral absolutes" with "a great feeling" that emphasizes a "mature bitterness."[7]

He Who Must Die became my shock weapon in my young Catholic activist days. It was with great sophomoric delight that I would challenge Sunday-only Catholics in parlor discussions with Dassin's revolutionary Christ. I felt compatible with Dassin's Christ figure, especially since I was also in the business of revolution, albeit on a smaller scale.

My next encounter with the Marxist Jesus was Pier Paolo Pasolini's classic *The Gospel According to St. Matthew. The Gospel* is simply the finest cinematic portrayal of the Christ story. It was directed by a known Marxist and homosexual, who was tragically murdered in the mid-1970s. But unlike Dassin's provocative Christ, Pasolini followed closely the text of Matthew's gospel. However, he shaded the performances and the settings to show more socioeconomic than theological disparities between Christ and the luxurious Pharisee priests and Roman conquerors.

Like Dassin, Pasolini, for the most part, used real people rather than actors; for example, an actual leper appears, as well as a man with a crippled leg. The effect is to give authenticity to a story that has been told too often and too badly. Pasolini's tale is both populist and sacred. *The Gospel* is also "quite complicated" and multilayered in meaning. The nuanced political subtext never overwhelms the main religious experience, but it is there nonetheless. In a conversation with Pat Jordan, managing editor of *Commonweal*, he exulted in the beauty of the film, calling it the "greatest Christ story on film."[8] Watching this two-and-a-half hour black-and-white movie again, I concur. Despite the incredibly slow pace, one becomes mesmerized.

Among his exquisitely crafted scenes, Pasolini gives us Salome's dance without advance notice. We see a beautiful pubescent girl in radiant finery accompanied by her mother, enchanting Herod in a rather simple dance. Her innocence and youth on the cusp of blooming captures Herod, rather than an exotic performance. The dance is incidental. Salome represents wealth and John the Baptist poverty, making for a startling contrast.

Neither Dassin's nor Pasolini's version of the Christ fable was greeted with hostility. Not so were the depictions of "the sexual Christ." The first cinematic foray into Christ's sexuality was quite mild, but it alarmed many of the faithful and was a dangerous film to watch in some theaters. Martin Scorsese, a former seminarian, had long wanted to film another of Kazantzakis' novels, *The Last Temptation of Christ*. I had read the novel when it was published in the late 1960s and found it an interesting, if less than riveting, speculation.

Kazantzakis had presented, as the most appealing of Jesus' temptations, a fictional reverie on the cross. Jesus dreams of reinventing his life as an ordinary man with a wife and children, unburdened by his divine agony to redeem humankind. Certainly, this temptation would have been a most powerful one.

Scorsese's film was hampered by a low budget and poor acting by some notable Hollywood stars, although Willem Dafoe gave a memorable performance as Jesus, a character he was to recycle in a number of other films. There were soft-core sexual scenes in the film. Unfortunately, *The Last Temptation* was simply a bad film cinematically. Nonetheless, when I viewed it in Virginia Beach, home of born-again Christians and Pat Robertson's religious empire, armed guards searched the movie patrons before entering, fearing violence to the screen.

But Scorsese had established the "sexual Jesus" for a large audience. It was but one more step—albeit a giant one—to extend that "sexual Jesus" into a homosexual Christ figure. The task was left up to the Tony Award-winning New York dramatist Terence McNally and his play *Corpus Christi*. Happily, after more than forty years, once again I had a shock weapon with which to lacerate homophobes and conventional Christians.

Despite his admonitions to the contrary, Terence McNally wrote an in-your-face play that was more of a play of ideas than the moving, heartfelt dramas of Dassin and Pasolini. From his Catholic upbringing, McNally was evidently conflicted with his homosexuality and Catholic doctrine. He describes *Corpus Christi* in the published edition as "more a religious ritual than a play."[9] *Corpus Christi* is a contemporary play set in the Texas town of the same name. McNally mixes it with the key dramatic events in the New Testament, updated.

But *Corpus Christi* is less a "religious ritual" than a play of ideas, and one that is not especially well fleshed out. McNally's polemical purpose is to show homosexuality as being part of our divinity. He writes in the preface to the play that his central assumption is that "if a divinity does not belong to all people, if He is not created in our image as much as we are created in His, then He is less a true divinity for all men to believe in."[10]

So his Christ figure is actively gay. There are two plot devices that establish McNally's argument: one wherein the Christ figure named Joshua (although the disciples bear their biblical names) has a homosexual relationship with Judas, who betrays him because he cannot possess Joshua fully; and the other device wherein Joshua is condemned to death by the priests and Romans because he has married two of his disciples who are gay.

Joshua's blasphemy, upon which the priests anchor their argument, is not that Joshua claims that he is the Son of God, but that, as the high priest says to Judas, "you're the Son of God as well." The divine within us is not an article of faith among Roman Catholics as much as it is among the American transcendentalists, Ralph Waldo Emerson and Henry David Thoreau. Nevertheless, despite its faults, *Corpus Christi* performs a service by further expanding Christ's humanity without detracting from his divine nature. The play is neither blasphemy nor sacrilege, but neither does it have the sacred quality of Pasolini's *The Gospel of St. Matthew*.

All artistic symbols lose power in time. If I were to fictionalize a res-urrected Christ among us today, I would depict him as a black homeless man with mild retardation, who—yes—is gay. For my understanding of Jesus is that, if he would return, he would be living on the margins of society, since his divine plan is to overturn the worldly establishment both theologically and materially.

NOTES

1. *Time*, December 29, 1958, p. 50.
2. John McCarten, *New Yorker*, January 10, 1959, p. 111.
3. Ibid., p. 110.
4. Philip Hartung, "Many Things to Many People," *Commonweal*, January 2, 1959, p. 363.
5. Ibid.
6. Robert Hatch, *Nation*, January 17, 1959, p. 60.
7. Ibid.
8. Interview with Pat Jordan, New York City, April 12, 2000 (telephone).
9. Terence McNally, *Corpus Christi* (New York: Grove Press, 1998), p. viii.
10. Ibid., p. v.

Reflections on a Modernist Canon

I decided to revisit some of the classic literary and philosophical masterpieces which influenced me in my formative years. Among the literary masterpieces I reviewed were the first major novels that made me realize that literature was a vibrant art practiced by living people—Ernest Hemingway's *A Farewell to Arms* and Jack Kerouac's *On The Road*. My philosophical baggage contains William James's *The Varieties of Religious Experience* and Albert Camus's *The Myth of Sisyphus*. No book has moved me more on social issues than George Orwell's *The Road to Wigan Pier*. My question is, then: Do these classics resonate with me as much now as they did a half century ago?

Once the door to classic works was opened, I discovered many important and influential books. Were I to be stranded in some desert island or woods, my list would now be different. I would choose to accompany me these novels: Gabriel García Marquez's *One Hundred Years of Solitude* (my current favorite author), William Kennedy's *Ironweed*, and Toni Morrison's *Beloved*. I have rediscovered John Dewey's *Democracy and Education* and *Art as Experience* for philosophy, and been imbued with the psychologist Howard Gardner's *Frames of Mind: The Theory of Multiple Intelligences*, and Carol Gilligan's *In a Different Voice: Women and Psychological Development*. I maintain a constant love for the poems of Allen Ginsberg and devour the spate of recent biographies on the abstract expressionists. The work of the African American sociologist

William Julius Wilson has been extremely provocative. I am not sure whether I have moved on from a Hemingway-Kerouac-Orwell-Camus axis but whether these authors have formed a mainframe for a certain modern sensibility.

I was attracted to the philosophy of William James by the most brilliant professor at Fordham, Robert Pollock. (Pollock was to be one of three Fordham professors to whom I dedicated my book *Teacher Politics*). Pollock taught graduate courses in philosophy, and I was given permission as a senior to attend his course on American philosophy. Pollock was a Jewish convert who had graduated from Harvard and was personally familiar with the great philosophers in America's golden age of philosophy—the Harvard coterie of James, Josiah Royce, George Santayana, and Alfred North Whitehead. His classes resembled a jazz session, with improvised insight and inspiration imbedded in a nearly indiscernible philosophical melodic order. Unfortunately his publication output was small, but it was choice—the quality being high. His difficulty in being published, his friends claimed, was that he was too liberal for the Catholics and too Catholic for the liberals. Pollock was the intellectual star of the Fordham faculty. I was in awe of him.

As a member of the elite American Civilization program, I was required in my senior year to complete a thesis, the length and quality to be the equivalent of a graduate master thesis. I decided to write my thesis on "William James and the Religious Experience." Pollock was affiliated with the American Civilization program and agreed to guide my senior thesis.

Although in awe of this scholarly master, I was bold enough to replicate Gertrude Stein's examination in William James's psychology class at Harvard. Stein simply refused to answer the genius professor's examination questions, preferring to write on another subject. At Pollock's final exam, I decided to offer *him* some of my own knowledge (but careful to mention the Stein/James precedent) by writing an essay on the history of jazz. Pollock gave me a B-plus on the exam and, for the course, a small admonition for my transgression. But he took me aside later to encourage me to be a writer, since he found both the jazz essay and the senior thesis of interest. I was thrilled.

William James as a psychologist/philosopher had good reason to study religion. His father was obsessed with religion—though not the institutional variety—and he transmitted his passion to his five children, whereby one observer felt "the James home a sort of church."[1] Both James and his son William had touched the depths of despair, which they felt had a religious basis. Son William's description of this despair, which accompanied his nervous breakdown as a medical student in Germany, is arguably the most famous in all of the pathological literature. In a "state of philosophical pessimism and general depression," William "without any warning" was overcome with a "horrible fear of my own existence." An image of a catatonic mental patient flashed through his mind, and he was beset with a terror in which he felt *That shape am I.* The result was that "the universe was changed for me altogether," he wrote, and "was like a revelation." William concluded that this "melancholia had a religious bearing." He is the first philosophical existentialist.

Varieties still carries freshness about it. James pays tribute to philosophers (such as Spinoza, Kant, Schopenhauer), theologians (Catholic and Protestant), writers (such as Leo Tolstoy, Walt Whitman, and Robert Louis Stevenson) but it is in his innumerable case studies that we get a psychological perception of the religious experience. The philosopher of experience values experience over abstract rational thought. He is clear in defining religion as "the feelings, acts, and experiences of individual men in their solitude, so far as they apprehend themselves to stand in relation to whatever they may consider divine."

James approached religion as a psychologist and told his audience, when presenting his lectures at the University of Aberdeen in Scotland in 1901, that he was "neither a theologian, nor a scholar learned in the history of religion." Yet *Varieties* was the first and perhaps, as one academic wrote, "the most influential book written on religion in the twentieth century."[2] The Protestant theologian Martin Marty demurs, considered *Varieties* "a classic," but one that was "too psychological to have shaped most religious inquiry and too religious to have influenced much psychological research."[3] In rereading *Varieties*, I disagree with Marty's estimation. I find the book to be a crossover study, rich in its literary quality and sound in its qualitative methodology of case studies. In a sense, James sought to defend religion. He was an unorthodox believer in a finite God in a developing pluralistic universe. Yet James had little personal exchange with a deity, having "no living sense of commerce with a God." He simply saw the need.

Varieties is well organized, the product of a highly structured philosophical mind. And it is gracefully written. William James was the psychologist who wrote like a novelist; the remark was forever to be repeated. His brother Henry James was the novelist who wrote like a psychologist. The sections that had initially attracted my interest were on "the sick soul," "saintliness," and "mysticism."

Looking back, I realize that many of my intellectual heroes were existentialist in one manner or another. Hemingway was a great influence on the French existentialists, such as Camus and Jean-Paul Sartre, with his two classic, early—and best—books, *The Sun Also Rises* and *A Farewell to Arms.* His prayer to nothingness, "Our Nada who art in nada give us this day our daily nada" could have been written by either Camus or Sartre. The characters in *The Sun Also Rises* are spiritually dead, and the lovers in *A Farewell to Arms* have found a darkness in life. William James's spiritual breakdown in *The Varieties of Religious Experience* is the same kind of death. And Jack Kerouac is now being hailed as "America's existential hero" for his depictions of marginal men outside the pale.[4]

Camus was a hero of mine. His existential philosophy combined with his activism as a resistance fighter during World War II, as well as his graceful writing, attracted me to him. I was not as enamoured of his novel of ideas, *The Stranger* or *The Plague*. Compared to the most serious American fiction, I considered his novels to be more philosophical tracts than great stories. But his political and moral philosophy was a lightning rod for young Americans entranced with French existentialism. *The Myth of Sisyphus* held the most power for me, although I also found *The Rebel* to be a fine introduction to a new and exciting mind travel.

Rereading *The Myth of Sisyphus* (my first full-length introduction to Camus), I am struck by how much of his thought I have unconsciously appropriated. I read *The Myth* because it is a philosophical treatise on suicide.

"There is but one truly serious philosophical problem," Camus writes, to open *The Myth*, "and that is suicide." He then proceeds to discard suicide as a plausible alternative for the new "absurd man" who is confronted with the contradiction of life, death, and a loss of heavenly eternity. Along the way Camus strikes a familiar chord for anyone who has had an emotional and philosophical depression. "There is no sun without shadow," he writes, with uncommon eloquence, "and it is essential to know the night." This emotion was fictionalized by Hemingway and to a lesser extent by Kerouac.

But in this "unintelligible and limited universe" what "is absorbed is the confrontation of this irrational and the wild longing for clarity whose call echoes in the human heart." According to Camus, humankind wants certainty about God's existence and the promise of a heavenly eternity. Consider this passage from *The Myth*:

I want everything to be explained to me . . . The mind aroused by this insistence seeks and finds nothing but contradiction and nonsense . . . The world itself, whose single meaning I do not understand, is but a vast irrational. If one can only say just once: "This is clear", all would be saved.

What saves French existentialism from being a pale imitation of the existentialism of Martin Heidegger and Karl Jaspers, of course, is not the diagnosis of the philosophical malady, but the prescription for the cure: action. For metaphysical nothing, one proceeds to work for the improvement of society. In short, Camus—and Sartre—were *philosophes engagés*. There is a long tradition of *philosophes engagés* in French history, dating back to Voltaire. Camus was editor of *Combat*, the French resistance newspaper during the Nazi occupation. He wrote *The Myth* in 1940 during the height of Nazi oppression, at the tender age of twenty-seven. He wrote that "great revolutions are always metaphysical." They may start with "social criticism," but they are ultimately rooted in the question of how God could permit suffering and injustice.

For the man of action, the absurd man, who can live with the contradictions of life and death, Camus believes that there is no need to justify one's existence. "The absurd man," Camus argues, "has nothing to justify." On this point we part company. For Camus, there is neither guilt nor original sin.

His metaphor for life, then, is the Greek Sisyphus myth. Sisyphus is condemned to forever roll a huge boulder up a hill, only to have it roll down again as he reaches the top. He must eternally repeat the exercise. The myth has several interpretations, but for Camus it signifies a dignity although it is a life without final outcomes, without eternal rewards.

The absurd argument does not resonate with me today as powerfully as it did when I was young. In the age of a new millennium, with the explosion of knowledge in science and the research in moral development by American scholars such as Lawrence Kohlberg and Carol Gilligan, *The Myth of Sisyphus* appears somewhat dated. But I see again how much of an intellectual debt I owe Camus.

It was a great joy when *Kirkus Reviews* assigned me to review Camus's essays collected in *Resistance, Rebellion and Death* shortly after he died in 1960. But of the twenty-three essays on topics of Nazism, the Algerian and Hungarian revolts, capital punishment, and the like, I was particularly disappointed by Camus's position on the Algerian uprising. Although born and raised in Algeria, Camus failed to side with the Arab movement for Algerian independence. He equivocated, revealed his deep sympathies for the colonial French. I considered it a betrayal of his moral ideals that he had carved out in his philosophy. I was not alone. His fellow existentialists, Sartre and Simone de Beauvoir, among others, condemned him for his position.

Even a relative unknown from Massachusetts, John F. Kennedy, had declared as early as 1956 his support for Algerian independence. I met Kennedy that year when we were both on a small plane out of Boston headed to Portland, Maine, he to a Maine Democratic Convention, I to visit my Aunt Emerilda. I complimented him on his courageous and lonely senatorial endorsement of Algerian independence.

Still, I muted criticism of Camus in my review, as I was still basking in the halo of one of the twentieth century's great men. I wrote that:

Biographically speaking, there is nothing as definitive concerning a man's life as the asides he speaks—to himself or while facing an audience . . . This is precisely what this book is. It does not explain Albert Camus. It reveals him . . . Certainly this is the most important book written about Camus, by one who knows him best.[5]

I was to revisit Camus thirty-eight years later when I wrote a short piece on his unfinished autobiographical novel *The First Man*. Then, I mainly looked at the intellectual and mentoring debt he owed to a schoolteacher in Algeria who enabled him to translate his intellectual gifts through school in order to escape poverty. Camus had written a letter of thanks to the schoolteacher upon receiving the Nobel Prize in literature. The letter was reprinted in an Afterword by Camus's daughter. My piece, "A Teacher's Legacy," was first printed in Education Week and later reprinted in the op-ed section of The Chicago Tribune.

Much of Hemingway stills travels well. My serious introduction to him was *A Farewell to Arms*, which I read in my junior year in college. *A Farewell to Arms* remains a classic love story as well as a subtle antiwar tract. In the Hemingway character, Lieutenant Frederick Henry, we have a war hero who continually questions heroism, war, and, as Camus points out, ultimately the metaphysical question of God's existence. Initially Henry does not believe in love or God—but he pursues both and finds both, though not without experiencing a death of spirit like that which attracted the French existentialists. This death of spirit also pervades *The Sun Also Rises*, but that book is seriously marred by Hemingway's homophobia and anti-Semitism, which are absent from *A Farewell to Arms*. Both books deal with major themes, yet the antiwar novel has a seamless quality.

A Farewell to Arms is still a beautiful read. It consists of two classic themes interwoven in one: a novel about the insanity of war, and a touching love story. Rereading the book nearly a half century later, I am still moved by its power to speak forcefully about war, love, and God.

The Hemingway hero, Lieutenant Frederick Henry, is an existentialist character. He finds the world absurd. He moans that

> That was what you did. You died. You never had time to learn. They threw you in and told you the rules and the first time they caught you off base they killed you.

A subtext to the novel is a metaphysical query about God. Henry has trouble sleeping nights. In response to an older Italian's comment that he had perhaps "outlived my religious feeling," Henry replies that "my own comes only at night." The first character Hemingway introduces in the novel after the protagonist is a young priest. The priest tells Frederick that "you do not love God," to which Henry replies "no," but "I am afraid of him at night sometimes." Throughout the novel Henry intellectually spars with the priest, delighting in his company. The novel is sprinkled with conversations between Henry and his comrades about God.

When his love, Catherine, lies dying after a misbegotten childbirth, Henry asks her if she wants to see a priest. She declines, only wanting Henry at her bedside because, as the old Count points out, love is also "a religious feeling."

Catherine also approaches the affair psychologically damaged. Her longtime engagement to a young man ended after eight years, when he was killed in the war. She is slightly off mentally. She tells Frederick that, when she met him, "I was nearly crazy. Perhaps I was crazy."

Neither Frederick nor Catherine begins the relationship in love. Henry admits to his comrade Rinaldi that he does not love Catherine when he first courts her. On her part Catherine is somewhat resistant to Henry's advances. But they do fall passionately in love. For Catherine, Frederick becomes "my religion." Henry is so motivated by love as she lies dying that he prays over and over to the God he suspects may not exist, "please, please, dear God, don't let her die."

A Farewell to Arms is arguably Hemingway's best book. All wars and all loves and all metaphysical wrestlings with God can be substituted for the time periods in this World War I novel: World War II, Korea, Vietnam. Perhaps of all my literary influences, Hemingway remains the strongest.

I was surprised in rereading *On the Road* how good it is. Unfortunately, through the years I had absorbed all the criticism of Kerouac that his novels were jejune and more typing than writing. I had stopped defending him in my mind. I clung to my early admiration of his work. His persona fit most of the culture stars I was obsessed with: romantic, tragic, alcoholic, all dying prematurely.

On the Road is carefully and elegantly written. It is a descent into hell from a writing angel (Sal Paradise) who is a participant-observer of the travails of young men and women born of the nuclear age—the age of absurdity. From the first lines in the book Kerouac strikes an existential theme.

I first met Dean not long after my wife and I split up. I had just gotten over a serious illness that I won't bother to talk about, except that it had something to do with the miserably weary split up and my feeling that everything was dead.

On that existentialist note Kerouac proceeds on his "pilgrim's progress" back and forth across the United States, full of hope that "somewhere along the line I knew there'd be girls, vision, everything; somewhere along the line the pearl would be handed to me." Instead, in his journey into night, he is confronted by, "rising from the under-

ground, the sordid hipsters of America, a new beat generation that I was
slowly joining."

What was the attraction of these "sordid hipsters" for Kerouac? Their
rage to live despite an absurd world. Kerouac explains:

The only people to me are the mad ones, the ones who are mad to live, mad to
talk, mad to be saved, desirous of everything at the same time, the ones who
never yawn or say a commonplace thing, but burn, burn, burn like fabulous
roman candles exploding like spiders across the stars and in the middle you see
the blue center light pop and everybody goes "Aww!"

Of course this is the second most famous Kerouac passage after the lyrical ending of *On the Road*, when he thinks of Dean Moriarty sitting at
sundown "on the old broken-down river pier" in New Jersey musing on
the beauty of America.

But Kerouac never loses his perspective as a writer. The antihero of
the novel, Dean Moriarty, is "a sideburned hero of the snowy West" who
was, on the one hand, "simply a youth tremendously excited with life"
but who was also, on the other hand, a "con-man." Kerouac ends his
pilgrimage to heed the advice of a "tall old man with flowing white hair"
with "a pack on his back" hitchhiking along with Kerouac, instructing
him to *"GO MOAN FOR MAN."* This Kerouac does by writing his novel,
a twentieth-century Dante's *Inferno* softened by Christian compassion
and Buddhistic belief in reincarnation.

On the Road exploded America's consciousness, and thanks to *Time* and
Life magazines, the most popular of their day, with their constant ridi-
culing of the Beat writers, Kerouac and Allen Ginsberg became overnight
cult stars, albeit ones who were outside the pale of mainstream society.
Time was also the magazine that insulted Jackson Pollock by calling him
"Jack the Dripper," and its sister magazine *Life* poked fun at Pollock by
calling him facetiously, "America's Greatest Painter."

The excitement generated by Kerouac in the Village was electric. I
recall that when Peter Martin, who knew Kerouac from his *City Lights*
days in San Francisco, mentioned to me that Kerouac was in the Village
that night, chills would run up my spine. Kerouac would often visit the
Cedar to hook up with de Kooning for a pub crawl. De Kooning loved
the company of writers, although he was not especially fond of the Beat
writer's work. Kerouac liked de Kooning, but not modern abstract expressionist art. I would always miss Kerouac at the Cedar, sometimes
by only a day.

The Catholic liberal discussion group, the Walter Farrell Guild, asked
me to speak one night in 1959 on the Beat Generation writers at the Hotel
Edison, on 44th Street and Eighth Avenue. The audience was full of
Catholic Worker activists and hippies.

I wrote about Kerouac twice. Two months after he died in October of 1969, I was chosen to be one of *Commonweal* magazine's Christmas book critics. I took the occasion to have as my first choice *Satori in Paris*, not only because I wanted to eulogize Kerouac, but because I had made my first trip to Paris after my first book was published. I wrote that "Kerouac exploded my consciousness in the 50's" and that "being a French Canadian from a similar New England town, I found he best explained me to myself."[6] Moreover, I found that Kerouac was in the "great religio-literary tradition of Melville, Whitman, and Hemingway."[7]

My second foray into Kerouac was an essay for my hometown literary supplement. In an essay on Kerouac's Lowell novels, I wrote that Kerouac dealt with his French Canadian heritage and that "he was the first (and only) major American writer of French-Canadian descent."[8] It was an admiring portrait. The Lowell novels dealt with Kerouac's roots in New England and, although charming in themselves, lacked the power and sweep of his road novels, which I wrote were "to alter the consciousness of America." Regarding the Lowell series, I concluded that "if anyone desires to know what it is like growing up French Canadian in New England during the first half of this century he should consult these three novels (*Vision of Gerard, Doctor Sax* and *Maggie Cassidy*)."

The crucial part of French existentialism, as I have mentioned, is its jump from metaphysical despair to activism. So it made perfect sense for me, to move easily into social action from depression, and from my Catholic humanist tradition to seek to justify my existence—redemption—through radicalism. My favorite book in my social activism days was George Orwell's *The Road to Wigan Pier*.

Parts of *The Road to Wigan Pier* consist of a beautiful read. Orwell's description of life among the miners in northern England is stark, branding one's compassion like a hot fire. The book was commissioned by the Left Book Club, a socialist organ published in 1937, in the depth of the Depression, which had nearly 40,000 readers. Orwell divided his book into two parts: one a depiction of life among the poor, and the other a tract expressing his left-sectarian critique of socialism and English socialists. The latter has little meaning except as a historical footnote.

Orwell was middle class, born out of wedlock. At a very young age he was a police officer in British Burma. He found that, toward the end of his five years, he "hated imperialism" and "was serving with a bitterness." He concluded in Orwellian convoluted logic that "in order to hate imperialism you have got to be part of it." His was a St. Paul's conversion to socialism, from oppressor to ultra-pure socialist, the enemy turned most ardent convert. In short, a left-sectarian.

As a former left-sectarian, I do not agree with Lenin's characterization of left-sectarianism as an "infantile disorder," but I understand Orwell's position. Paradoxically, I tend to be revolted by Orwell's brand of left-sectarianism, probably because he became a chief enemy through distortion by the right wing of his novels *Animal Farm* and *1984*. I still feel that way forty years later.

But as a chronicler of poverty in *The Road to Wigan Pier* and *Down and Out in Paris and London*, Orwell has no peer. His sharp novelistic powers detect among the poor "the smell of poverty." A foreward to the book was deemed necessary by the socialist editors to dismiss much of Orwell's views. Victor Gollancz, one of the three editors of the Left Book Club, would argue that not only was Orwell mistaken about English socialists being "stupid, offensive and insincere," but about the accusation that "the working class smells."[9] Gollancz would attempt damage control by stating that "Mr. Orwell is exaggerating violently."[10]

Orwell was ambivalent about the poor. On the one hand, he was revolted by their poverty. On the other hand, he romanticized the poor. Consider these two very different sentiments from *The Road to Wigan Pier*:

The real secret of class distinctions . . . is summed up in four frightful words . . . *The lower classes smells* . . . As a child, one of the most dreadful things I could imagine was to drink out of a bottle after a Navy (working man).

On the other hand, Orwell in the same book would paint an idyllic, romantic picture of the working poor:

In a working class home . . . you breathe a warm, decent, deeply human atmosphere which is not so easy to find elsewhere. I should say that a manual worker . . . has a better chance of being happy than an "educated" man. His home life seems to fall more naturally into a sane and comely shape.

I found in my visits to the homes of poor Hispanics a distinct smell of poverty due to poor diet, different food odors, and slum housing. My approach to working with the poor, like Orwell's, smacked of a bourgeois paternalism. My colleagues and I were "cadre," or as Orwell proclaimed, "in almost any revolt the leaders would tend to be people who could pronounce their aitches." We were occasionally broke, but never poor. Being poor meant having neither the economic nor the psychological means to deal with what we called in the 1960s "the power structure."

I did not share Orwell's romanticization of the poor. Michael Harrington in *The Other America*, and other scholars of my time, had clearly shown that mental illness, crime, brutality, abuse, and all the other pathologies were more pronounced among the poor than among the middle class. Nevertheless, other romantics such as Jack Kerouac, would have another version of poverty. In *On the Road*, Kerouac yearned as he walked "the lilac evening" in Denver slums with "every muscle aching . . . wishing I were a Negro" as he "passed the dark porches of Mexican and Negro homes" where he heard "soft voices," saw "occasionally the dusky knee of some sensuous gal" and the "dark faces of the men," and "little children sat like sages in ancient rocking chairs." Black Panther Eldridge Cleaver, in *Soul on Ice*, considered this passage "remarkable" because Kerouac found positive things in black poverty, whereas the sociologists continually harped on the pathological negatives.[11] I could be counted among the latter.

What of *The Road to Wigan Pier*? The book still carries power. One testament to its vibrant message is that it is still in print, in quality paperback. Orwell wrote his tract for the already converted choir, and thus was given a pulpit to preach to his congregation to make them better socialists. But his encounter with poverty, passionately recorded, has meaning for those who have yet to be converted as well.

The Road to Wigan Pier still merits classic status. The only American counterpart to Orwell's tome is Michael Harrington's *The Other America*. The difference between the two books is that Orwell brought to his subject the art of the novelist, whereas Harrington brought the skill of the polemicist. Moreover, Harrington's book was intended for policymakers in Washington, D.C., to jolt them into action, which it did.

NOTES

1. William James, *The Varieties of Religious Experience* (New York: Penguin Books, 1982), p. xii.

2. Ibid., p. vii.

3. Ibid.

4. *The Jack Kerouac Collection*, CD Liner Notes, Los Angeles, California: Rhino Records, Inc., 1990 p. 17.

5. Maurice R. Berube, Review of Albert Camus's *Resistance, Rebellion and Death*, Kirkus Reviews, December, 1960. Reprinted in *Book Digest 1961* (New York: H.W. Wilson Co., 1962).

6. Maurice R. Berube, "Christmas Book Critics Choices," *Commonweal*, December 5, 1969, p. 311.

7. Ibid., p. 312.

8. Maurice R. Berube, "Kerouac Wrote of His Heritage," *Lewiston Journal Magazine*, February 26, 1977, p. 1.

9. George Orwell, *The Road to Wigan Pier* (New York: Harcourt Brace, 1958), p. xiii–xiv.

10. Ibid., p. xiii.

11. Eldridge Cleaver, *Soul on Ice*, (New York: McGraw Hill, 1968), p. 72.

Bibliography

BOOKS

Ashline, Nelson F., et al. *Education, Inequality, and National Policy*. Lexington, Massachusetts: Lexington Books, 1976.

Assante, Molefi Kete. *Afrocentricity*. Trenton, New Jersey: African World Press, 1990.

Bell, Terrell H. *The Thirteenth Man: A Reagan Cabinet Memoir*. New York: Free Press, 1988.

Berube, Maurice R. *The Urban University in America*. Westport, Connecticut: Greenwood Press, 1978.

Berube, Maurice R., and Marilyn Gittell, eds. *Confrontation at Ocean Hill-Brownsville*. New York: Praeger, 1969.

Bérubé, Michael. *Public Access: Literary Theory and American Cultural Politics*. New York: Verso, 1994.

Bruner, Jerome. *The Process of Education*. New York: Vintage Books, 1960.

Carmichael, Stokely, and Charles V. Hamilton. *Black Power: The Politics of Liberation*. New York: Vintage Edition, 1992.

Camus, Albert. *The First Man*. New York: Vintage Books, 1996.

Chubb, John E., and Terry M. Moe. *Politics, Markets and American Schools*. Washington, D.C.: The Brookings Institute, 1990.

Cleaver, Eldridge. *Soul on Ice*. New York: McGraw Hill, 1968.

Dewey, John. *Art as Experience*. New York: Capricorn Books, 1934.

———. *How We Think*. Boston: D.C. Heath, 1933.

During, Simon, ed. *The Cultural Studies Reader*. 2nd ed. London: Routledge, 1999.

Fish, Stanley. *Professional Corrections: Literary Studies and Political Change*. Oxford, England: Clarendon Press, 1995.

Friedman, Benjamin M. *Day of Reckoning*. New York: Random House, 1988.

Gardner, Howard. *Extraordinary Minds*. New York: Basic Books, 1997.

Gates, Jr., Henry Louis, and Cornel West. *The Future of the Race*. New York: Vintage Books, 1996.

Giltin, Todd. *The Twilight of Common Dreams: Why America is Wracked by Culture Wars*. New York: Metropolitan Books, 1995.

Gross, Beatrice, and Ronald, eds. *The Great School Debate*. New York: Simon and Schuster, 1985.

Harrington, Michael. *Fragments of a Century*. New York: Saturday Review Press, 1973.

Harrison, Helen A., ed. *Such Desperate Joy: Imagining Jackson Pollock*. New York: Thunder's Mouth Press, 2001.

Hirsch, E.D., Jr. *Cultural Literacy*. New York: Houghton Mifflin, 1987.

———. *Cultural Literacy: What Every American Needs to Know*. New York: Vintage, 1988.

Hofstadter, Richard. *Anti-Intellectualism in American Life*. New York: Knopf, 1963.

Horgan, John. *The End of Science*. New York: Addison-Wesley, 1996.

Isserman, Maurice. *The Other American: The Life of Michael Harrington*. New York: Public Affairs Press, 2000.

Jacoby, Russell. *The Last Intellectuals: American Culture in the Age of Academe*. New York: Basic Books, 1987.

James, William. *The Varieties of Religious Experience*. New York: Penguin Books, 1982.

Jameson, Fredric. *The Crucial Turn: Selected Writings on the Postmodern, 1983–1998*. London: Verso, 1998.

Kadushin, Charles. *The American Intellectual Elite*. New York: Basic Books, 1974.

Katz, Michael. *Class, Bureaucracy and the Schools*. New York: Praeger, 1972.

———. *Reconstructing American Education*. Cambridge, Massachusetts: Harvard University Press, 1987.

Kingsley, April. *The Turning Point: The Abstract Expressionists and the Transformation of American Art*. New York: Simon and Schuster, 1992.

Lang, Berel, ed. *The Death of Art*. New York: Haven, 1984.

Lucas, Christopher J. *American Higher Education: A History*. New York: St. Martin's Griffin, 1994.

McCoy, Charles Dean. *The Education President*. Austin: University of Texas Press, 1975.

McNally, Terence. *Corpus Christi*. New York: Grove Press, 1998.

Michael, John. *Anxious Intellectuals: Academic Professionals, Public Intellectuals, and Enlightenment Values*. Durham, North Carolina: Duke University Press, 2000.

Moore, M.G., and G. Kearsley. *Distance Education: A Systems View*. Belmont, California: Wadsworth Publishing Co., 1996.

Naifeh, Steven, and Gregory Smith. *Jackson Pollock: An American Saga*. New York: Clarkson N. Potter, 1989.

Nelson, Stephen James. *Leaders in the Crucible: The Moral Voice of College Presidents*. Westport, Connecticut: Greenwood Press, 2000.

Orwell, George. *The Road to Wigan Pier*. New York: Harcourt Brace, 1958.

Potter, Jeffrey. *To a Violent Grave: An Oral Biography of Jackson Pollock*. New York: Pushcart Press, 1985.

Ravitch, Diane. *The Great School Wars: New York City, 1805–1973, A History of the Public Schools as Battlefield of Social Change*. New York: Basic Books, 1974.

———. *Left Back: A Century of Failed School Reforms*. New York: Simon and Schuster. 2000.

———. *National Standards in American Education: A Citizen's Guide*. Washington, D.C.: The Brookings Institute, 1995.

———. *The Revisionists Revised*. New York: Basic Books, 1977.

———. *The Troubled Crusade: American Education, 1945–1980*. New York: Basic Books, 1983.

Reedy, George. *Lyndon B. Johnson: A Memoir*. New York: Andrews and McNeel, 1982.

Reutter, Jr., E. Edmund, and Robert R. Hamilton, eds. *The Law of Public Education*, 2nd ed., Mineola, New York: Foundation Press, 1976.

Rosovsky, Henry. *The University: An Owner's Manual*. New York: W.W. Norton, 1991.

Sheehy, Gail. *Character: America's Search for Leadership*. New York: William Morrow and Co., 1988.

Thurow, Lester C. *The Zero-Sum Society*. New York: Penguin Books, 1981.

Wilson, William Julius. *The Truly Disadvantaged*. Chicago: University of Chicago Press, 1987.

ARTICLES

Bentsen, Cheryl. "Head Negro in Charge." *Boston Magazine*, 1990.

Berube, Maurice R. "Christmas Book Critics Choices." *Commonweal*, December 5, 1969.

———. "The Dumbing Down of the Candidates." *Virginian Pilot*, August 26, 1992.

———. "The End of School Reform." *Commonweal*, April, 1972.

———. "Kerouac Wrote of His Heritage." *Lewiston Journal Magazine*, February 26, 1977.

———. "Review of Albert Camus's, *Resistance, Rebellion and Death*." Kirkus Reviews, 1960.

Bérubé, Michael. "Public Academy." *New Yorker*, January 15, 1995.

———. "Why Inefficiency Is Good for Universities." *Chronicle of Higher Education*, March 27, 1998.

Berman, Ronald. "Scholastic Aims and Political Battles." *New York Times Sunday Book Review*, September 18, 1983.

Bornstein, Rita. "Back in the Spotlight: The College President as Public Intellectual." *Educational Record*, Fall, 1995.

Boynton, Robert. "The New Intellectuals." *Atlantic Monthly*, March, 1995.

Carr, Sarah. "Is Anyone Making Money on Distance Education?" *Chronicle of Higher Education*, February 16, 2001.

Cohen, David. "What Standards for National Standards?" *Phi Delta Kappan*, June, 1995.

Donato, Ruben, and Marvin Lazerson, "New Directions in American Educational History: Problems and Prospects." *Educational Researcher*, November, 2000.

Eisner, Eliot N., "Standards for American Schools: Help or Hindrance?" *Phi Delta Kappan*, June, 1995.

Enarson, Harold, "Review of Maurice R. Berube, *The Urban University in America*." *Journal of Higher Education*, January/February, 1980.

Featherstone, "The Politics of Education," *New York Times Sunday Book Review*, June 18, 1978.

Finn, Jr., Chester E., "What Ails Education Research." *Educational Researcher*, January/February, 1988.

Fukuyama, Francis, "The End of History?" *The National Interest*, Summer, 1989.

Gardner, Howard, "The Need for Anti-Babel Standards." *Education Week*, September 7, 1994.

Goodlad, John I., "The Vision Thing: Educational Research and AERA in the 21st Century, Part 2." *Educational Researcher*. June/July, 1997.

Hanusek, Eric A., "The Impact of Differential Expenditures on School Performance." *Educational Researcher*, May, 1989.

Hartung, Philip, "Many Things to Many People." *Commonweal*, January 2, 1959.

Herbert, Bob, "In America." *New York Times*, August 28, 2000.

Herbert, D., "Model Approaches to Arts Education." *Principal*, March, 1998.

Hedges, Larry V., Richard D. Laine, and Rob Greenwald, "Does Money Matter? A Meta-Analysis of Studies of the Effects of Differential School Inputs on Student Outcomes." *Educational Researcher*, April, 1994.

Hesburgh, Theodore, *Chronicle of Higher Education*.

Holden, Stephen, "Splashed Across Life's Canvas, Dripping." *New York Times*, September 30, 2000.

The Jack Kerouac Collection. CD liner notes. Los Angeles, California: Rhino Records, Inc., p. 17.

Kimmelman, Michael, "Frame by Frame, an Action Film Dripping with Art." *New York Times*, December 10, 2000.

———. "How Even Pollock's Failures Enhance His Triumph." *New York Times*, October 30, 1998.

Koch, James V., "How Women Actually Perform in Distance Education." *Chronicle of Higher Education*, September 11, 1998.

Levine, Arthur, "The Soul of a New University." *New York Times*, March 13, 2000.

Levine, George, "Education as a Reflex of a Politics." *New York Times Sunday Book Review*, May 12, 1974.

Lewis, Anne E., "An Overview of the Standards Movement." *Phi Delta Kappan*, June, 1995.

Melamida, A. et al., "Painting by the Numbers: The Search for a People's Art." *The Nation*, March 14, 1994.

Miller, Matthew, "$140,000—And A Bargain," *New York Times*, Sunday Magazine, June 13, 1999.

Mosle, Sara, "The Fourth R." *New York Times Sunday Book Review*, August 27, 2000.

Neufeldt, Harvey, "Review of Maurice R. Berube, *The Urban University in America*." *Educational Studies*, Summer, 1979.

Parker, Walter C., Akira Ninomiya, and John Cogan, "Educating World Citizens:

Toward Multinational Curriculum Development." *American Educational Research Journal*, Summer, 1999.

Ravitch, Diane, "Adventures in Wonderland: A Scholar in Washington." *The American Scholar*, Autumn, 1995.

———. "Lawrence A. Cremin," *The American Scholar*. Winter, 1992.

———. "Multiculturalism: E Pluribus Unum." In Paul Berman, ed., *Debating P.C.*, New York: Laurel, 1992.

Schrag, Peter, "The Education of Diane Ravitch." *The Nation*, October 2, 2000.

Shanker, Albert, "What Are They Selling?" *New York Times*, June 25, 1995.

Slaughter, Jane, "Interview with Henry Louis Gates, Jr., *Progressive*, January, 1998.

Wang, Margaret C., Geneva D. Hartel and Herbert J. Walberg, "Toward a Knowledge Base for School Learning." *Review of Educational Research*, Fall, 1993.

Wicker, Tom, "Bush's Report Card." *New York Times*, October 6, 1989.

REPORTS

Alliance for the Arts. 1993. *The Arts as an Industry: Their Economic Importance to the New York-New Jersey Metropolitan Region*. New York: The Port Authority of New York and New Jersey.

Bennett, William J. *American Education: Making It Work*. Washington, D.C.: U.S. Department of Education, April, 1988.

Carnegie Foundation for the Advancement of Teaching. *School Choice*. Princeton, New Jersey, 1992.

Ikenberry, Stanley O, and Terry W. Hartle. *Taking Stock*. Washington, D.C.: American Council on Education, 2000.

Larson, E.O. *American Canvas: An Arts Legacy for Our Communities*. Washington, D.C.: National Endowment for the Arts, 1997.

Lazar, Irving, and Richard B. Darlington. *Lasting Effects After Preschool*. Ithaca, New York: Cornell University Press, October 1978.

National Commission on Excellence in Education. *A Nation at Risk: The Imperative for Educational Reform*. Washington, D.C.: U.S. Department of Education, 1983.

National Women's Studies Association. *Liberal Learning and the Women's Studies Major*. College Park, Maryland: University of Maryland, 1991.

New York State Task Force on Minorities. *A Curriculum of Inclusion*. Albany: New York Department of Education, July, 1989.

Old Dominion University, *The Village of the 21st Century*. Norfolk, Virginia: Old Dominion University, 2000.

Sheftal, Beverly Guy. *Women's Studies: A Retrospective*. New York: Ford Foundation, June, 1995.

Stimpson, Catherine R., with Nina Kressnor Cobb. *Women's Studies in the United States*. New York: Ford Foundation, 1986.

U.S. Department of Education. *America 2000: An Education Strategy*. Washington, D.C.: U.S. Government Printing Office, April 18, 1990.

NEWSPAPERS/MAGAZINES

Education Week, November/December, 1999.
Nation, January 17, 1959.
New Yorker, January 10, 1959.
New York Times—August 31, 1987; December 6, 1989; March 14, 1994; August 25,
    1996; September 28, 1996; December 15, 1996; February 19, 1997; April 14,
    1997; October 5, 1997; May 23, 1998; October 30, 1998; December 11, 1998;
    September 30, 2000; December 10, 2000.
Time, December 29, 1958.

UNPUBLISHED MATERIAL

Bush, George, "Address to Congress," New York *Times*, February 10, 1989.
Bush, George, "Remarks by the President," The White House Office of the Press
    Secretary, Charlottesville, Virginia, September 28, 1989.
Brochure, Northeastern University, Boston, Massachusetts, 2000.
Old Dominion University, "Doctor of Philosophy in Urban Services—Proposal
    to State Council of Higher Education in Virginia," Norfolk, Virginia, 1979.
Rudenstine, Neil, "Commencement Address," Harvard University, June 8, 2000.
Rupp, George, "Commencement Address," Columbia University, June 5, 2000.
Urban Affairs Association, "Institutional Members," University of Delaware, Jan-
    uary 24, 2001.

INTERVIEWS

Berube, Maurice R. Interview with Pat Jordan, New York City, April 12, 2000
    (telephone).
Berube, Maurice R. Interview with Janet Lyon, University of Illinois in Cham-
    paign/Urbana, March 2, 2001.
Berube, Maurice R. Interview with Diane Ravitch, New York City, December 4,
    2000.

TELEVISION

Lamb, Brian, Interview with Diane Ravitch, *Booknotes*, C-SPAN Television, Tran-
    script, September 15, 2000.
Lamb, Brian, Interview with Henry Louis Gates, Jr. *Booknotes*, October 9, 1994,
    C-SPAN Television Transcript.
Hunter, Madeline, in Dwight Allen's Television Course "Educational Reform,"
    Old Dominion University, April 10, 1988.

VIDEOS

deAntonio, Emile. *Painter's Painting*. Video. New York: New Video, 1972.
Kadish, Reuben. *Jackson Pollock: Portrait of an Artist*. Video. London: R.M. Arts,
    1987.

Index

About the Author

MAURICE R. BERUBE is Eminent Scholar of Education at Old Dominion University, Norfolk, Virginia. He is the author, co-author, or editor of nine earlier books, including *Eminent Educators* (Greenwood Press, 2000) and *American School Reform* (Praeger, 1994).